BACHELOR'S JAPAN

BOYE DE MENTE

BACHELOR'S JAPAN

CHARLES E. TUTTLE CO.: PUBLISHERS
Rutland, Vermont & Tokyo, Japan

Other Books by Boye De Mente

Bachelor's Hawaii
Some Prefer Geisha: The Lively Art of Mistress-Keeping in Japan
The Tourist and the Real Japan
How Business is Done in Japan
Japanese Manners & Ethics in Business
Once a Fool: From Tokyo to Alaska by Amphibious Jeep
Oriental Secrets of Graceful Living
Faces of Japan: 23 Critical Essays
The Japanese as Consumers: A General Description of Asia's First
　Mass Market (with Fred Perry)

Representatives

For Continental Europe:
BOXERBOOKS, INC., *Zurich*

For the British Isles:
PRENTICE-HALL INTERNATIONAL, INC., *London*

For Australasia:
PAUL FLESCH & CO., PTY. LTD., *Melbourne*

For Canada:
M. G. HURTIG LTD., *Edmonton*

Published by the Charles E. Tuttle Company, Inc.
of Rutland, Vermont & Tokyo, Japan
with editorial offices at Suido 1-chome, 2-6, Bunkyo-ku, Tokyo

Copyright in Japan, 1962 by Boye De Mente

All rights reserved

Library of Congress Catalog Card No. 67-11428

Standard Book No. 8048 0052-9

First printing, 1967
Fifth printing, 1970

PRINTED IN JAPAN

This book is dedicated to the women who make Japan a man's paradise. Without them, the country would have fewer friends.

Contents

CONTENTS

BACHELOR'S JAPAN

Message To Bachelors

WHILE THE essence of bachelor entertainment is more or less the same the world over, attitudes concerning the conduct of bachelors differ widely—with the result that bachelor manners and techniques also differ. Everyone knows, for example, that French bachelors behave in a distinctly French way, and that British bachelors have their own peculiarities. But this poses no special problem for the Western man-about-town in England or France for the first time because he knows what to expect and how to behave in most situations.

The first-time visitor in Japan, however, is generally not familiar with the peculiar rules governing Japanese society, especially the ones applying to sensual pleasure, and is therefore at a considerable disadvantage. This book is an attempt to catalog and explain the more important attitudes, manners, and techniques currently prevailing in Japan, as well as provide visiting travelers and businessmen with useful "inside" information on the *mizu shobai* or entertainment trades in Tokyo and other Japanese cities.

Before one can appreciate Japan's unique "float-ing world," of which the Geisha are now only a small part, it is necessary to know something about the position of sex in Japanese culture, a key factor in the development of this distinctive sphere of Japa-nese life.

Sex to the Japanese has traditionally been one of several "human feelings" which, so long as it was kept in its place, was something to be engaged in regularly and completely. Unlike most Westerners, the Japanese have never considered sex evil, and as a result sensual pleasure in itself was never the sub-ject of moral censorship.

There was a traditional separation between a man's erotic pleasure and his duty as a husband and father. Marriages were arranged, and a man's obli-gation to his wife was a major family obligation that had no connection with erotic experience. This came under the heading of minor pleasure, and was gener-ally engaged in outside the home, more or less like the American husband stopping off for a beer after leaving his office in the evening.

There were, however, different sex standards for men and women. So long as it did not interfere with any of the other areas of his life, the Japanese male's indulgence in sex for the sake of pleasure was con-trolled by his pocketbook, rather than his moral con-science. Women who did not belong to the entertain-ment world were ostensibly expected to be virtuous, although it was common for young ladies of rank to have lovers, and there was in practice considerable license among women of the lower classes.

Japanese attitudes toward sex are changing— *thanks* to Western influence. But there is still enough difference to make an interesting—and often baffling —contrast for the visiting foreigner.

Bachelors are reminded that the rules are subject to change everytime the game is played. Mere possession of this book does not guarantee success. It will, however, get you over the threshold, so to speak, and give you signals and suggestions on how to proceed from there. As far as the ball-carrying is concerned, that's up to you.

I would have been both pleased and relieved to publicly acknowledge the contributions made to this book by several of my friends and colleagues, but their modesty and unselfishness, along with some serious threats of mayhem, precluded me from doing so. Being now married, and therefore unable to claim *all* the credit myself, I am forced to renounce responsibility for any compromising statements alluding to firsthand experience on the part of the writer.

Boye De Mente
Tokyo, Japan

1 / The Pleasure Capital Of The World

WRITERS have long portrayed France as the world's best bachelor country. If this was ever true—and it may have been at one time—it is true no longer. Most experienced, well-traveled bachelors now agree that no country can compare with Japan in the things that really count.

One purpose of this book is to remedy to some extent this failure to accord the fabled land of the Geisha proper recognition as the world's leading purveyor of bachelor pleasure. As a matter of fact, before going into the what, when, where, and how portions, I think it would help to establish Japan's pre-eminence in the field by very briefly reviewing just the capital's history of catering to pleasure-seekers—whether they were bachelors or not.

Tokyo, as all good students of Japanalia know, made its formal debut into Japanese history in 1457 as *Yedo* (or *Edo*), when Ota Dokan built a fortress there (forerunner of the Imperial Palace) to protect the northern frontier. At that time, *Yedo* was a tiny

fishing-farming village surrounded by marshes, la-
goons and seven low hills. It remained no more than
a military outpost and stopover on the road to Nikko
and Aizu until 1590 when Ieyasu Tokugawa, founder
of Japan's last great feudal house, received the eight
provinces in the surounding area in fief and made
Yedo his headquarters.

In 1603 when the Tokugawa family became su-
preme in Japan, Yedo was made the administrative
capital of the country, and the population and size
of the city exploded. In addition to 80,000 retainers
making up the Tokugawa "house," Ieyasu forced the
nation's 300 territorial barons to build homes in
Yedo and keep their families there as hostages to
ensure their own good behavior. Osaka merchants
were also induced to set up shop in the new capital.

Into this lusty young city poured artists, entertainers, and the forerunners of women who were to
create a new genre of pleasure, a "floating world,"
that was to give its name to an art and spread its
influence as far away as Europe.

The center of this "floating world" were the redlight districts, great and small, that sprang up
throughout the city. On the fringes, along every road
leading into *Yedo,* were hundreds of "tea houses"
staffed with girls who provided the steady stream
of travelers with more than just tea to satisfy their
thirst.

Within a few years after the city became the
administrative capital of the country, the towns-

people began gathering in an area on the outskirts (present-day Nihombashi) called *Yoshiwara* (Reedy Plain), to view plays and dancing. Before long, the area became a notorious redlight district; and the Government subsequently closed it down.

In 1617, an enterprising *Yedo*-ite managed to obtain a license from the authorities, re-opened the area, and was a success overnight. To help promote business—and in a flash of the type of inspiration so typical of the Japanese—he began to write *Yoshiwara* with ideographs that meant "Happy Field" rather than Reedy Plain.

His success was short-lived, however, as about this time bathhouses in *Yedo* proper began to feature young female attendants who "entertained" as well as bathed their clients. These bathhouses rapidly became gay resorts on a stupendous scale, and the *Yoshiwara* became a reedy plain again.

After several years of profitable operation, one of the most famous of the bath-with-house establishments made the tactical error of setting up right in front of the mansion of an important territorial baron, and as a result the bath girls and their masters were put out of business in 1650.

Hundreds of these girls gathered in an area about two miles northeast of *Yedo* Castle (present-day Asakusa) and began plying their trade without benefit of soap and water. Following a series of great fires in 1657 and 1658 that nearly destroyed the city, the original Yoshiwara (which had never completely disappeared) was moved, bag and baggage, to this small area, and the name went along. The sight of all the girls and their attendants in colorful costumes moving to their new location is described in many Japanese stories of this period as a spectacle never to be forgotten.

By 1700, the walled-in *Yoshiwara* was known as *Fuyajo,* or "Nightless City," and was surely the pleasure capital of the world. Each night the streets and houses were filled with men of all descriptions, including *samurai* (Japan's privileged, sword-carrying warrior class) in disguise, artists, jugglers, pickpockets, wealthy merchants, and writers seeking themes for their novels and plays.

The *Yoshiwara* became a distinct town—almost a country within itself—with manners and ethics entirely its own. A special etiquette was observed between visitors and courtesans, who were divided in rank, with the highest ones waited upon by many richly attired servants. On special days, the girls put on their finest kimono and made elaborate, much heralded processions through the streets of *Yedo*—a practice that is still followed by several Geisha districts in Tokyo today.*

As the years of the Tokugawa era unfolded, bringing decade after decade of peace after some 300 years of almost continuous warfare, the people's will

* During the *Yoshiwara's* heyday, the girls couldn't leave the area except in a procession to see cherry blossoms at Ueno, or to visit their dying parents.

to pleasure regained its own as a primary drive, and the fleshpots and tea ceremony flourished side-by-side, overflowing.

This great surge of passion for beauty, extravagance, and worldly pleasures reached its peak around 1700, by which time the haughty *samurai* had lost most everything but their pride, and this was often in hock to some enterprising merchant. By law the *samurai* could still kill with impunity any common man who so much as used disrespectful language to him, but as his livelihood came to depend more and more upon the despised commoners, he gradually learned to sublimate his arrogant pride.

While the *samurai* were thus left with their dignity and high social position, it was the *cho-nin,* the lowly townspeople, who had the money and the fun. Revelry and drinking became the pastime and the mark of every man. Proud fathers often introduced their sons to the delights of the gay quarters as soon as they reached puberty, and drinking was not only a custom but a duty, which was enthusiastically sanctioned by society.

In this atmosphere, the gay quarters became palaces of luxury as well as pleasure, attracting women of the greatest beauty and skill, and men of all classes and occupations. To the townspeople, *Yedo was the greatest city on earth, and a being could ask for no more than to be born a man in Yedo, eat bonito at New Years, and visit the gay quarters even at night* (the latter part referring to the fact that during this period *samurai* were not supposed to enter the entertainment districts at night, resulting in them going in disguise).

Most of the art and literature of Japan during this era which treated of human factors was conceived, nourished, and brought to bloom in the heady air of *Yedo's Yoshiwara,* the largest of the many entertainment areas.

Except from the viewpoint of Western morals, which are preached but not practiced, there was nothing vulgar about the gay quarters of *Yedo,* for despite the spectacle of voluptuously rich silks and bright lacquers which characterized the areas, the daily and nightly affairs of the patrons and pleasure girls were conducted with more refinement and grace than anywhere except possibly the Palace of Versailles.

Not since the days of the Pompeians had worldly pleasure played such an important role in the life of a city. And out of this fusion of pleasure-seeking grew the world of the *mizu-shobai,* literally "water-business," or the business of catering to men in pursuit of ephemeral pleasure.

Tokyo's *Yoshiwara* (and its counterparts in Kyoto, Osaka, and other cities) not only continued to fluorish throughout the long years of the Tokugawa reign (1603–1868), they also survived the Restoration in 1868 when the feudalistic Tokugawa Government was toppled and the Emperor was restored as the head of the nation.

In fact, it was only in 1957, after a history of 340 years, that the *Yoshiwara,* along with all of Japan's legal gay quarters, was given the *coup de grâce* by a group of women in the Diet. On that last night before April 1, (Fool's Day) 1957, I went with several friends to watch the *Yoshiwara* die. Much of it, of course, was already dead. The elaborate rules of etiquette and rank, the sophistication and dignity, had already weakened until they were hardly discernable.

The measure outlawing legalized prostitution actually went into effect a year before this, on April 1, 1956, but a year of grace was provided for the girls and house madames to find another occupation. Before the end of this year, about ninety percent of the girls in the licensed areas had relocated or disappeared, and a large percentage of the houses had been converted to coffee shops, bars and inns. So the last night was something like staying at the carnival grounds after the crowd leaves, and watching the place fold up.

2 / Successors To The Redlight Districts

THE DEATH of the legal redlight districts, which for centuries had personified Japan's pleasure sphere, did not mean the end of the *mizu shobai,* however. There is a great deal of debris in the "floating world" now, and its waters are streaked with mud, but here and there the charm and fascination and even grace of the old world still manage to shine through.

It remains today one of the most important "industries" in each of Japan's largest cities, and in more than a hundred cities, like Atami about two hours south of Tokyo and Beppu near Fukuoka, it is the major industry.

The main character of the present-day *mizu-shobai* is its emphasis on speed at the expense of propriety. In form, it is divided up into areas and categories. For the sake of convenience, I list these as cabarets (including what everybody incorrectly calls night clubs*), bars, ryokan or Japanese style inns, hotels, Japanese style restaurants, bathhouses, and coffee shops, not necessarily in that order.

What might be called the lineal successors to Japan's legal gay quarters are the thousands of bars and cabarets where customers may pick up partners, and the accompanying hotels, apartments, and inns used as houses of assignation.

You can, in fact, immediately discern the business and social position of both the girls and their customers by their "place of meeting" and "place of return-

---

* According to Japanese law, night clubs are not allowed to have hostesses, so all of Japan's famous nightspots featuring beautiful girls, bands and entertainment (Copacabana, Hanabasha, New Latin Quarter, etc.) are legally cabarets. There are presently some 400 cabarets in Tokyo and only thre night clubs: the Vesta Club in Shibuya, the Happy Valley in Ikebukuro and the Grand Asakusa in Asakusa. For the record, there are some 2,450 bars (cafes in the eyes of the law) registered in Tokyo.

ing." Girls catering to laborers, students, and the lowest paid office employees, work out of the lowest class bars. On top of the heap, as far as most Japanese customers are concerned, is a large group of girls working in small, exclusive, high-priced cabarets in the entertainment areas of Japan's major cities.

These girls, sophisticated and expensively groomed, cater to company executives on liberal expense accounts, and use the hundreds of ryokan (euphemistically termed "love hotels" by the Japanese press) as their nightly bivouac. In Tokyo, for example, Sendagaya, Yoyogi, and Harajuku areas are especially noted for the large number of such ryokan, but they abound all over the city.

The biggest problem facing the 96 "love-inn" owners in Sendagaya, according to the *Sunday Mainichi,* is how to spend the tremendous profits they have piled up. Most of them, the weekly magazine said, eventually resort to squandering large sums on trips abroad. Other tidbits of information provided by the affluent inn-keepers: 70 per cent of their regular customers are business executives with office girls; one-twentieth of their customers are married women with lovers; 80 per cent of the women who frequent the inns with men do so for money; very beautiful women are often masochists, and are provided with an extra large room and a rope; not many foreign men/Japanese women couples visit the inns —but when they do the men are charged double the going rate and the extra money is given to the girls as a kickback; foreigners frequently sneak out without paying their partners.

In between these two classes are the run-of-the-mill bars and cabarets that live off the earnings and expense accounts of petty bureaucrats and company functionaries.

Way up in the stratosphere, above all but the most famous Geisha, movie stars, and models, are the beautiful, glamorous, mink coat and diamond-digging girls in Tokyo's Copacabana, Hanabasha, New Latin Quarter and, lower by a few hundred feet, the Shirobasha and the Queen Bee, etc., and similar clubs in Osaka, who mine the apparently bottomless pockets of foreign businessmen and tourists with a skill that would have turned Robin Hood as green as his livery.

When the Anti-Prostitution Law went into effect on April 1, 1957, there were over 50,000 licensed redlight district houses in operation, staffed by 260,000 registered "fun girls." An extensive survey in 1966 reveals that in approximately 70 per cent of these old districts the lights are back on again in a variety of shades. The most conspicuous feature now is the role of the *tateba*, or the procurers who stand between the prostitutes and their patrons.

Depending on the city and the area, the *tateba* may be taxi drivers (who get as much as half of the girl's fee), former redlight house owners, gangsters who operate call-girls rings under the guise of "Sightseeing Guide Clubs", and old women who tout for street-girls organized and controlled by underworld gangs. There are some 25 of these "guide clubs" in Kita-Kyushu City, for example, all of which operate in close cooperation with inns generally run by ex-brothel keepers.

Another gambit now used by former redlight girls is to attach themselves to restaurants as "delivery girls", in order to have an excuse to visit guests in inns.

In the Osaka area, many former good-time girls now double as waitresses and maids in beer parlors. These parlors operate on the "one set" system, meaning one bottle of beer and a small plate of tidbits for a set price. A customer who orders three "sets" is allowed to take one of the waitresses out. Osaka playboys who prefer a more direct approach, cross the Kanzaki River to Amagasaki City, where prostitution is practiced with less police interference. The former licensed redlight districts were in the center of the city, an area swarming with students. So as an "educational consideration" the ex-brothel keepers now operate in the outskirts of the city as inn-keepers.

In Nagoya, ryokan have replaced the former redlight houses almost entirely. The girls are listed as maids. Gifu City, not far from Nagoya, has the reputation of being the most open city in central Japan. The two most common routines there are for bar and cabaret hostesses to accompany guests to a nearby "neon bath" (Turkish bath), or for the guest at an inn to simply ask for a girl.

Tokyo's once fabulous Yoshiwara redlight district in Asakusa is certainly no more. But there is still action going on—all controlled by gangsters. To avoid breaking the malleable Anti-Prostitution Law, *Odenya* (push-cart food sellers) are used as procurers. As long as a potential patron approaches within 15 feet of the *Odenya* he is legally a customer of the food cart, and the operator cannot be prevented from talking to him.

In addition, at least 50 of the old redlight house-turned inn employ prostitute-masseuses (pan-ma). Maids in these Yoshiwara ryokan often attempt to solicit passing men by calling to them through windows and from behind partly closed doors. The old Yoshiwara also has its quota of Turkish baths, guide clubs, and free-lancers.

Many of the former houses in Tokyo's well-known Shinjuku 2-chome district are now "nude studios". Each "studio" has from two to six very pretty young girls who stand in the doorway or lined up in front of the studio. The girls attempt to attract business by calling to passing men, occasionally taking them by the arm or some other appendage to press home their point—very much like the girls did when the area was a licensed redlight district.

During the street sales pitch the girls give potential customers the idea that anything is possible if the customer will just pay the fee and step inside. Once inside one of the tiny cell-like rooms with a customer the girl undresses down to her panties and then asks the customer for an additional sum of money to cover "special poses". If the customer comes through, she redresses, takes the money out, returns and undresses again.

There are signs on the wall explaining that the customer is not supposed to touch the girl, and that she should not be asked to assume improper poses. Of course, the cynical and the experienced find it hard to really believe that nothing low-down or licentious takes place in these "studios".

According to a self-styled expert on Japan's playboy activities, the 15 best fun areas in the country are (in the order of ease of contact and inexpensiveness) : Yanagase (Gifu City), Daikumachi (Takamatsu), Dobusaku-ue (Nagoya), Gionkoji (Hachinoe), Matsugane (Utsunomiya), Daimon-ura Oyafuko-dori (Hakodate), Shijokawara (Kyoto), Shinyanagicho (Hakata), Sonezaki-ura (Osaka), Ueno (Tokyo), Tenmon-ura-dori (Kagoshima), Susukino-dori (Sapporo), Nishikimachi Asakusagai (Kofu), Imaike (Nagoya), and Yurakucho (Hamamatsu).

3 / *How Modern Night Life Began In Japan*

BEFORE 1920, nearly all night life in Japan was provided by Geisha houses (actually restaurants—with private rooms—that call in Geisha) and the traditional redlight districts that dated back to early To-kugawa days. There were no night clubs, cafes, or cabarets comparable to what existed in the West at that time.

By the early 1920's, however, only the very wealthy could afford to patronize Geisha houses, in which the atmosphere and service remained traditional, and the customer had little or no control over how much he was going to pay for it. Furthermore, the redlight districts, which still catered to the working man, had degenerated to the point where they no longer offered sufficient satisfaction to the man seeking release from everyday cares. Modern living had forced them to put sex on an assembly line basis, and there was no time for frills.

In addition, several thousand Japanese had been abroad by this time, experienced the clubs and cafes of Paris and other Western cities, and upon returning home had begun to spread the desire for some type of night life more suited to modern Japan.

First came shops serving coffee. Styled directly after French shops, they were naturally called cafes. Before long, they began serving alcoholic drinks. In a few years, these establishments developed into what were to be known as cabarets. Their history was brief, however, as Japan's military government suppressed them in 1937.*

When the Pacific war ended in 1945, Japan's caba-

* A few, catering exclusively to the military, were allowed to remain in business.

ret operators were in no position to take up where they had left off in 1937. In addition to being destitute, they were restricted from engaging in the sale of foods and liquors by various Occupation regulations.

These restrictions did not apply to Chinese, Koreans, Americans, or other foreign nationals in Japan, many of whom within weeks after the war ended were making tremendous profits through blackmarketing and other illegal activities.

Large numbers of these newly affluent foreigners took advantage of their special status under Occupation laws to buy up land and buildings in choice spots in Tokyo, Osaka, and other cities, and open bars, clubs, and restaurants. Most such businesses in these cities today are still owned by Chinese and Koreans, the Americans having been squeezed out.

These first clubs and restaurants that sprang up in postwar Japan catered almost exclusively to military and foreign clientele and their Japanese girl friends. It was not until mid-1948 that Japanese-owned clubs catering primarily to Japanese customers began to appear.

Another phenomena precipitated by the American military occupation of Japan was the development of club and cabaret entertainment. In prewar Japan, cabarets rarely if ever had floor shows, and Western style club entertainment was practically unknown.

The U.S. military changed all this. Every unit had its club, and every club attempted to feature some kind of floor show at least twice a week. Show business in Japan suddenly became big business, and anybody with the nerve to get up in front of a bunch of GI's could make money. A saying current during those early years was that even a *Chindonya** could make out as a night club act. In fact, the American Club of Tokyo actually did feature *Chindonya* as entertainment one time during this period.

These were the days when Izumi Yukimura, Chiemi Eri, Nancy Umeki and other top stars of today were teenagers learning their trade in front of rowdy GI audiences on the military club circuit.

The army clubs also brought the stripper to Japan. Before this period, not only had strip shows of the Western type been virtually unknown in Japan, the whole idea was foreign to the Japanese.

Japan had traditionally had its nudes in various forms, a flourishing pornographic industry, private sex shows, and other displays—some of them public— of an erotic nature. But the strip tease a la West was as amazing to them as the performance of one of their fertility rites would be to Bostonians if it were staged in Haymarket Square on Sunday afternoon.

From the military clubs, the strip show spread to the commercial clubs operated by Chinese, Koreans

---

* *Chindonya* are people, usually in groups of three, who dress in colorful Japanese costumes and parade about the streets playing various musical instruments and cutting humorous capers to advertise a newly opened shop or some coming event. The music they make is characterized by drum beats and the strident sound of flutes and trumpets.

and other foreign national nightclub entrepreneurs.

Some of the strippers came from the United States, some came from Australia and others were recruited locally. Many of those from abroad, especially those from the U.S., were hoary battle-axes that had been bumping and grinding for twenty years or more and could no longer make the grade back home.

Commercial clubs during this period wouldn't pay more than ¥30,000 (about $85) a night for a floor show, and since a stripper was the only entertainer that could carry a single act, the cult flourished.

In 1959, Tokyo's Monte Carlo club brought in an acrobatic team of seven girls and one man from Australia. Called the "Rudas Show" after the name of the owner of the act, the team was paid ¥100,000 ($278) a night, the highest fee ever paid for club entertainment in Japan.

Business at the Monte Carlo had been in a slump, and almost everybody in the field thought the management had gone crazy. But the show ran for four weeks and made money.

This put the marker on the already shrunken military market, and heralded the rapid rise of big-money show business on the open market in Japan.

Entertainers from half a dozen countries began flocking to this new gold field, where talent came last. There were also a lot of big names like Nat King Cole, who reportedly knocked down $25,000 a week during his sojourn here.

In the early months, entertainers came in as tourists. Immigration still hadn't recovered from the Occupation days when they had little or no authority, and Japan was a mecca for the fast-buck artist.

Finally, in 1958 a stripper from Mexico, whose act would have rekindled the Chicago fire, spurred the local officials to action. An investigation revealed that she was not supposed to be practicing her art. At a not too subtle suggestion from Immigration, she covered up her assets and left.

Immigration thereupon instructed all booking agents to report any foreign entertainers working in Japan, and in general tightened up on the import of foreign talent, requiring anyone who intended to perform here to have a special entertainer's visa and pay local taxes.

Removal of the excess profit-making slot machines from American military clubs in Japan finished them off as important buyers of club entertainment. In the meantime, top Japanese clubs had instituted a cover charge system to pay for the more expensive foreign shows. In the half-club half-cabarets in Tokyo's Ginza area, cover charges run from around $1.50 to $2.50, while the so-called night clubs in Akasaka charge from $3 to $4 per table. On special occasions, such as when top-name foreign entertainers are being featured, these clubs charge as much as $15 for a table.

Even though the supply of capable Japanese entertainers is now more or less adequate, foreign talent is still much sought after in Japan's *mizu shobai*—for a very interesting reason, according to an informant who should know.

"The average Japanese feels vastly inferior to Caucasian foreigners, and it is this inferiority complex that is primarily responsible for the continued success of foreign night club entertainers in Japan," says a top Japanese booking agent.

"Japanese audiences are incapable of judging the degree of talent displayed by a foreign entertainer, especially a singer, and therefore cannot fully appreciate a foreign act. Yet, such acts go over best because the Japanese like the feeling of being entertained by white people or foreigners," the booking agent continued.

"As a result," he added, "white entertainers command the highest fees in Japan's *mizu shobai,* regardless of the quality of their act. Negro performers get comparable fees only if they are a really big name. Filipinos, Chinese or other non-Japanese Orientals are the lowest paid of foreign entertainers."

4 / The Present-day "Floating World" In Tokyo

SINCE TOKYO is the gate through which most visitors to Japan pass, an up-to-date description of the "floating world" in this city is the most useful, and will serve at the same time as a general introduction to the *mizu shobai* throughout the country.

There are five large and famous entertainment districts in Tokyo that date from *Yedo* days, and one that began to flourish in the early 1950's. The five are in the Ginza, Shinjuku, Ikebukuro, Shibuya and Asakusa districts, and a sixth is in the Akasaka area, site of one of Japan's best-known Geisha districts.

The Ginza entertainment district, located in Chuo Ward* in the center of downtown Tokyo and made of an area measuring about a quarter of a mile in width and half a mile in length, is a "high-class" district. While Asakusa, about two miles northeast of the downtown area (where the historically famous *Yoshiwara* was located) is now considered "low-class." Class-wise, the other areas are in between in the order listed. Shibuya is about two miles southwest, Shinjuku is about two miles west, and Ikebukuro is about three miles northwest of downtown.

Until 1957, all of these areas except the Ginza included one or more large redlight districts and several bluelight (non-licensed) districts. (Altogether, there were 16 large redlight districts in Tokyo before prostitution became illegal in Japan in 1957). The six entertainment areas today are made up of hundreds of closely packed bars, cabarets, coffee lounges, Turkish baths, theaters, and

* There are 23 wards (boroughs) in Tokyo.

restaurants. There are, for example, 550 bars and cabarets on the Ginza alone. Asakusa's Rokku amusement center boasts 30 theaters.

One way of trying to visualize what these areas are like at night is to imagine a Coney Island crowd in an enlarged Greenwich village-type place in which the setting is contemporary Japanese—a fantastic conglomeration of gaudy neon signs continuously exploding into exotic Chinese ideographs and startling designs; almond-eyed Oriental girls in sweaters and tight capri pants, and occasionally beautiful kimono, milling around in narrow streets and alleys in droves; taxis gouging their way through solid masses of people; gangster-types in sport shirts and green hats lolling about... in a scene beyond the imagination and means of a Hollywood extravaganza.

In addition to the five big entertainment areas named, there are several dozen smaller ones, not counting the still flourishing Geisha districts.

Although few foreigners are ever invited to a Geisha house (you generally can't get in without arrangements made in advance by someone known by the house), there are some 45 listed districts in Tokyo. The three most famous are Yanagibashi, Akasaka, and Shimbashi. (Shimbashi also offers a large selection of low-class bars and cabarets.)

Other well-known Geisha districts in Tokyo are Yoshicho, Nihonbashi, Shitaya, and Negishi. The girls in Shimbashi stage spring and fall processions, while those in Yanagibashi appear in public only in the fall.

A wealthy New York playboy doesn't necessarily have to throw baskets of money away to keep the girls interested in him. The known fact that he has money is usually enough to keep him busy. But not so in the cameo paradise of the first-class Geisha world. Here the price of status comes high.

Before a man can expect to become known in the Geisha world and be given the deferential treatment reserved for important personages, he must spend at least ten evenings a month in a Geisha house and run up a bill of not less than a million yen ($2,778) each month for at least one year.

Even then, so ephemeral is this status that should he fail to visit the Geisha district for a single month, he is forgotten, and must start the whole process over again. It is just as well, perhaps, that most top Geisha houses would not think of catering to foreigners.

Akasaka, the Geisha area traditionally favored by Japan's top government leaders, has been gaining considerable stature in recent years as a general entertainment district catering primarily to foreigners. The area now includes several of the best clubs and bars in the city, and is also noted for fine restaurants specializing in Western as well as Japanese foods.

As a historical note, the first Western style restaurant in Tokyo was the Ryudo-ken, opened in Azabu in 1897 by Kikumatsu Okano. The restaurant is still in operation and is run by the founder's grandson. A branch by the same name is located near

Roppongi intersection, just above the **Akasaka** Geisha district.

According to the legal definition, there are only three night clubs in Tokyo, but people in the "floating world" make their own distinctions. In their eyes, a cabaret is a place where hostesses come with the table. The customer has a choice of girls if he wants to exercise it, but if he makes no selection, girls are assigned to the table by turns.

During the time they are waiting for customers, cabaret hostesses sit around anywhere, gossiping and entertaining themselves. Many unassigned girls join parties which already have a full quota of hostesses, just to pass the time.

Hostesses in cabarets also tend to dress in loud, conspicuous styles, to be noisy and playful. Their conversation with guests is as provocative or lewd as the customer wants it to be. The aim of every cabaret girl is to get as many customers as posible to ask for her, to select her as their *shimei** everytime they patronize the place because she gets a special bonus (shimei-ryo) for drawing the customer in. This fee, in turn, is added to the customer's bill, the amount depending more or less on what the traffic will bear.

Hostesses in cabarets and "night clubs" seldom if ever go by their given names. Many change names

* *Shimei* means "nomination". Shimei suru means to nominate or select a favorite girl as your hostess for the evening. The shimei system is also used in Turkish baths and sometimes in Japanese style restaurants.

every time they change clubs. Because of this and also because the girls tend to favor the same names, many cabarets assign numbers to their girls to avoid confusion, and the girls use the numbers for the same reason.

To help them entice customers back again, cabaret hostesses invariably have name cards that they pass out to guests. Many of the girls may also ask you to remember their number—because so many customers throw the cards away before getting home, and there is a better chance that they will remember a number longer than a name.

The more clever girls work up their own private gimmicks for luring customers back time after time. One common routine is to tell the man that he reminds them of their father. This hits the customer in his reverse Electra complex and he gets a deep psychological boost out of playing with his daughter-image.

Other girls give their customers perfumed handkerchiefs, or some other gift designed to accomplish their purpose. All of the girls give their guests the idea that if they want to they can make out.

In cabarets where the *shimei* system is in effect, experienced men-about-town suggest that you control your ego and not select especially pretty girls. Unusually attractive girls are invariably *shimei* for many steady customers, and they are constantly being called by someone else. If the cabaret is crowded, the girl may be dividing her time between several tables, with the result that she is available to you for as little as one-fourth of the time, depending on how many groups she is presiding over.

If you are a really big spender, however, and especially if there is a chance you will be a repeat customer, the girl may favor you at the expense of her other patrons.

All *shimei* are very much interested in keeping you as a regular customer, however, and they do their best to ring in a girl that pleases you when they are away from your table. Since most customers travel in pairs or small groups, whatever girl is called usually attaches herself to the one that appears to be the leader. But to protect her interests when she is called away, she tries to see that the "leader" doesn't get lonely while she is gone.

In "night clubs" on the other hand, hostesses are not automatically assigned to all customers who come in. The girls stay at the bar or in the background, and join tables only at the request of the customer. Furthermore, they are more conservatively dressed and are generally much more reserved in their behavior because a significant percentage of night club customers are foreigners who neither expect nor demand the rowdy atmosphere preferred by Japanese out on the town. Rates for hostesses in night clubs consist of a flat fee, usually around $2.75 per hour, regardless of whether you ask for a particular girl or not.

Night clubs also generally include full-scale dining

service—which very often is among the best in the city—because having a restaurant on the premises makes it possible for them to stay open later than cabarets.

Another significant difference between night clubs and cabarets is that girls working in night clubs have little or no chance to increase their income through *shimei* fees or by padding bills, and as a result many of them augment their earnings by engaging in extra-curricular activities with guests during their free time. The girls are selective and their price is high, averaging between twenty-five and a hundred dollars a night.

Others are married or living with boy friends, and a few are simply unavailable for their own private reasons.

Both night clubs and cabarets are supposed to close at 11 p.m.*, but most large cabarets stretch this out until around 11:30 and many of the smaller bar-cabarets manage to keep going until 2 a.m. or later by turning off all outside lights, closing all doors and pretending to be a private party. Night clubs also use this ruse. In addition, they have a sentry posted on every street leading to the club to watch for police patrols.

If a patrol is spotted and it becomes fairly certain it is headed for a particular club, all dancing stops, the hostesses disappear and the customers are herded

---

* Girls under 18, including geisha, are not supposed to work after 10 p.m. Police try to enforce this law in Kyoto, but nowhere else.

into the adjoining restaurant, which has no curfew. The giant *Mikado,* Tokyo's largest and most elaborate cabaret with over 1,000 hostesses, was originally a supper club designed to get around this curfew.

There is presently a movement underway among night club operators to get the curfew extended— officially for the benefit of tourists—but cabaret owners are opposing the plan because it would take more business away from them.

The only thing that would allay opposition from cabarets and induce the Government to agree to such a revision of the law would be for night clubs to give up the right to have hostesses on the premises. Since more than half of their attraction is provided by the girls, there is little chance this will come about.

Among other regulations affecting the entertainment world is one applying to public dancing in Tokyo hotels. A few years ago, the "morals" section of the Tokyo police department summarily informed all hotels that dancing on the premises was banned.

They gave as the reason: "Dancing between a man and a woman is bound to create a certain feeling of love which is more than likely to result in an undesirable act after the dance." This official insinuation that Tokyo's leading hostels were in danger of becoming houses came as a shock to the proprietors, since they had traditionally had the right to set their own standards for guests.

As is usual in Japan in any controversial situation, however, a visit to the police department by a delega-

remove their coat, loosen their tie, get drunk, sing, shout, use lascivious language, and play free with the tion representing the hotel owners resulted in a compromise. The regulation was changed to allow hotel guests to dance *with each other*. Guests are still not supposed to dance with partners or even friends who are not staying at the hotel.

In addition to this, all dance areas must be fully lighted. As a Japanese commentator said when the regulation was put into effect, "The inconsistency of the bureaucratic mind knows no bounds!"

For several years, most top hotels in Japan have frowned on non-Oriental guests entertaining lady friends in their rooms, but there is tacit approval (in practice) if both parties are Japanese.

Several managers of leading hotels in Tokyo admit privately that their facilities are indeed used as houses of assignation by Western guests—on such a prodigious scale, in fact, that should they attempt to prevent the practice the hotels might not survive the loss of patronage.

Older Japanese men, often referred to as "Meiji men" (a commonly used appellation for men born during the Meiji period—1868-1912), seldom patronize night clubs unless they are entertaining foreign guests or clients, or have been dragged there by Geisha or cabaret hostesses. The reason for this is that older Japanese men like to "relax" in traditional style when they go out drinking. This means they

girls. Any guest of a Meiji man who fails or refuses to reach this stage is considered insincere in that he doesn't show proper appreciation for his host. In other words, it is ill-mannered not to "forget all etiquette."

Since this type of behavior is frowned on in the name night clubs, Meiji men particularly but most Japanese men as well, are not attracted by them. Recently, however, more and more Geisha and cabaret girls have been prevailing upon their customers to take them to night clubs, and it is a common sight to see one or more Meiji men, ill-at-ease and their faces beet-red from drinking, with a covey of gaily dresed Geisha at such clubs as Tokyo's Copacabana or Hanabasha.

This Japanese preference for drinking places at which they can "forget all etiquette" accounts for the slow development of night clubs in Japan.

Most Japanese cabarets function more or less as semi-private clubs, and known patrons are allowed to charge their bills so long as a hostess, usually their *shimei,* accepts responsibility for collecting the debt.

The system varies slightly with different cabarets but it is generally this: Before a hostess can gain the right to allow her customers to charge their bill she must deposit anywhere from $556 to $2,777 of her own money with the cabaret. If at the end of the month, she hasn't collected all the bills for which she accepted responsibility, the sum outstanding is deducted from her deposit. If a hostess who has acted as a guarantor for a customer's bill skips out without collecting the account, she is blacklisted and no cabaret will hire her.

Generally, the hostess will telephone the customer employed by a smaller company at his office just before the end of the month, and remind him of the bill. Patrons who are slow in paying or appear to be trying to beat a cabaret out of a bill, leave themselves open for some very effective collection techniques.

The responsible girl will present herself at the customer's place of business and ask to see him. In the event the erstwhile customer tries to stall, or refuses to see her, she begins to act hysterical and demands to see his boss or some other high-level officer of the company.

She proceeds to cry and rave loudly about how trustworthy she thought so-and-so was, what a good company she thought he worked for, how she is being held responsible for his debts, etc. Not too many can withstand being put in his spot and pay up quickly. Or as it often happens, a fellow co-worker pays for them while they remain in hiding.

Having signing privileges at two or three of the more interesting cabarets can be very convenient if the visitor is going to be in Japan long (it is a highly respected status symbol) and the privilege should be protected if you want to maintain good relations with the *mizu shobai* girls.

Up until recently, the Japanese never mixed

eating with drinking. Eating was required to sustain life and was something to be finished as quickly as possible whereas drinking was something that came under the heading of pleasure. One never mixed these two areas of living.

Proper Japanese manners today still call for a strict separation of the two functions. Older Japanese who have not adopted Western manners are apt to be insulted if a guest begins to eat before the drinking is done, or continues drinking after he commences eating.

It is very common to see Japanese men in a restaurant order beer with their meal, and then let their food set and get cold while they take their time drinking. According to Japanese etiquette, once food has touched your lips you have stopped drinking.

This practice often upsets first-time foreign visitors when they are invited out to Japanese style dinners, because they think they are going to starve to death before the eating begins. Old hands at the game take this custom into account and fortify themselves with a pre-dinner snack whenever possible.

In Western style restaurants, the visitor doesn't have to worry about being conspicuous if he choses to eat and drink at the same time. But it is wise to keep this traditional custom in mind when you are a guest in typical Japanese surroundings.

The cabaret business in Japan is highly competitive. The keys to success and profit are the hostesses.

As a result, successful hostesses are in demand and bring a very high price.

Just as baseball scouts watch the minor leagues for future pros, hostess scouts keep close tabs on promising cabaret girls. When a girls works her "billings" up to half a million yen a month ($1,388) she becomes "hot" and other cabarets bid for her.

A girl who obviously has what it takes, and can take her customers with her, may be offered up to five or six thousand dollars to move to another cabaret. If she accepts the offer, a big lump of this bonus usually goes as her deposit to give her charging privileges at the new cabaret. When talking about their customers in this case, the girls do not refer to the patrons themselves but to their company. Miss "South," for example, may say that her customers are Mitsubishi Electric, Fuji Iron & Steel, etc.

The "Hollywood" of Japan's thousands of cabaret hostesses is Tokyo's Ginza district. It is the ambition of every professional hostess to get into one of the exclusive name clubs in this area.

Far from disliking a system which requires them to be bill collectors, the girls wouldn't have it any other way because they are able to pad their bills, thereby collecting from both ends. The girls know what their customers are good for by their company and their position, and sometimes with a helpful hint from the customer himself, since company employees regularly connive with favorite hostesses to milk extra money from their firm. They therefore base their bill on what they think the market will bear, rather than on what the customer actually drinks up or otherwise spends.

This system is old and well-entrenched, especially where large, well-known firms are concerned. On a prescribed day the girls submit a bill to the accounting section of the customer's company. If he is only of medium rank, the accounting department submits it to him or his superior for approval, and once it has been stamped, pays off.

If the customer is a top ranking executive of a large company, the head accountant will okay payment without ever bringing the bill to his attention. This gives the hostess an open door to increased earnings—and explains how some of them make $10,000 or more a year.

Another result of this situation is that cabaret girls are not very much interested in customers who pay cash, preferring instead the week-in week-out habitues on expense accounts. They point out that no matter how much money a customer has of his own, he is almost always reluctant to shell out a lot of it in cash. This particularly applies to foreign customers, the girls say.

On the other hand, Japanese company employees on expense accounts are spending money whose benefit they can't get any other way, so they spread it around lavishly—the companies preferring to spend their profits on entertainment in lieu of giving it to the tax office.

Cabaret hostesses prefer that reliable customers who are not spending company money also drink on the cuff, because this makes it necessary for them to visit the cabaret at least once a month in order to pay their bill; and the girls are usually able to see that they run up another bill before leaving.

Although most Japanese cabarets have set prices for their drinks printed on menus or posted where they can be seen, the customer's bill depends upon how long he is in the place, how many girls favor him with their company, and whether or not he is a known, steady customer, rather than on what he has to eat or drink.

The first two factors are fairly concrete and value received can pretty well be judged. The third consideration, however, tends to be arbitrary, and very often catches the uninformed visitor off guard.

It is the practice in a large percentage of Japan's cabarets, particularly in the small, exclusive type, to charge incidental customers from twenty to several hundred percent more than the steady-client rate. Their idea is that they are not obliged to give a stranger their best price, that he is fair game to be plucked for the benefit of known patrons.

The only way to avoid this siutation is to arm yourself with an introduction or go with someone who knows the place concerned and is accepted as a regular customer there.

"Bunny Girls" are the latest fad to hit Japan's *mizu shobai*. First introduced by the Suntory Osaka

Club in Osaka's Sonezaki-shimmachi district, the girls wear net tights set off by white tails, collars, and cuffs. The club and the bunny girls are a direct steal from Hugh Hefner's Playboy Clubs. Members pay an initial fee, then monthly dues. Prices are very low in comparison with other clubs, and members may bring their own bottles if they wish. The Suntory Osaka Club features several popular Japanese games —go, mah jong, and shogi—in addition to cards and dice. The bunny girls may join the members in playing but cannot sit with them as do ordinary hostesses.

In addition to cabarets and night clubs, different style salons are now the thing. In Osaka, for example, there are *Negligee Salons* (where the hostesses all wear negligees), *Furisode Salons* (where the hostesses wear old-style kimono with long sleeves), and *Ozashiki Salons* in which the patrons sit on tatami reed mat floors.

Many Japanese playboys who are not on expense accounts favor *nomiya* which are bars without hostesses. But often all the bartenders are pretty girls. The girls drink with customers and come out from behind the bar and sit with them if they are not busy. There is no charge for this sort of companionship, and the price of drinks in *nomiya* is low when compared to cabarets and night clubs.

Kobe has many such bars more or less exclusively for foreigners. Those identifiable by dim red and blue lights are usually for foreigners. In Tokyo, club rooms and lounges on top of some of the new posh hotels are beginning to compete with the low down bars and clubs. The roof-top lounge on one downtown hotel features young foreign girls dressed in attractive yukata as waitresses.

5 / Why Girls Are "Cool" In Night Clubs

THERE are other important differences between night clubs catering to foreigners and cabarets catering to Japanese, and the alert bachelor may want to keep these differences in mind.

Girls in foreign-oriented clubs are invariably more reserved, harder, and in many ways colder than the hostesses in strictly Japanese cabarets. This comes about primarily because of two reasons. The girls in "foreign" clubs are in more direct and much stronger competition with each other, and they lose the little-girl coquettishness so typical of un-Westernized Japanese girls, after a few months of exposure to foreigners.

The hostess in a Japanese cabaret, generally speaking, may have been in the business for fifteen or more years and have had a life of great misery and sorrow. Yet when a customer comes in she exudes childish gaiety, friendliness, and eternal happiness.

The average hostess in a club frequented mostly by foreigners, regulates her charm and friendliness by the amount of money the customer spends and the size of the tip she expects to receive. If she is among those who—through outside activities—earn $1,000 or more a month (about ten times as much as a skilled technician makes), she is prone to take on manners befitting a queen who condescends to let someone lay down the rug for her.

This type of behavior apparently impresses and pleases big-spending foreigners, but the idea of a girl behaving in this manner in a strictly Japanese cabaret is unthinkable. A hostess in a cabaret who displayed any signs of snobbishness or superiority would quickly become an outcast. The most successful girls in Japanese cabarets are those who combine good looks and wit with the ability to make Japanese men enjoy their company—which means a pliable, patient, and uncomplaining manner regardless of what they have to put up with.

Once someone has experienced this type of personality and behavior, it is difficult to be content with Westernized hostesses...when you are in a night club. When it comes to associating with hostesses during their off-duty hours, the Westernized girls have many advantages. They generally speak some English and know how to dress and behave in such a way that you won't be embarrassed or put in any other type of awkward position while with them in public.

In private, too, there are advantages, as the foreignized girl will be less likely to become exceedingly coy and babyish, both of which are standard characteristics for un-Westernized girls.

Foreigners who don't know and aren't particularly interested in why the "pure" Japanese girl behaves the way she does, often get themselves into frustrating and serious predicaments. I have known many cases in which a foreigner invited a young lady up or out to see his woodblock prints, and ended up either aching from the unrelieved presure or as far as he knew, guilty of some degree of rape.

Girls in the business, who are being paid night rates, will also often put on a act, either of innocence or fatigue, and get by with it more often than you would think. Where the pro's are concerned, the most effective solution is to demand your money back if you've already paid, or threaten to kick the girl out.

If it is between friends, it is often a subtle and complicated affair. It is a common practice for ordinary Japanese girls to go on weekend trips to spas with boy friends, and share the same room with them without intending to go all the way. They do it as a test. If the boy friends don't force them, and take it standing up, you might say, the girls accept this as proof of their genuine affection for them. Generally after this exercise, an intimate relationship follows within a very short period of time.

Not being up on the rules of the game, the foreigner thinks that since his invitation to spend a night together is accepted, everything else can be taken for granted. This may not be the case, however, particularly if the foreigner is going to be in Japan for quite some time and is actually an eligible bachelor.

If you are in Japan for only a temporary stay and the young lady in question knows it, you can be pretty sure that if she agrees to your proposal it gives you carte blanche. Bachelors in Japan on a long-term basis don't have it so clear-cut. There may be no sign until the moment of truth, although some girls may make a point of ordering separate sleeping mats, so there is nothing to do but play it by ear. Whatever the bachelor does he is usually safe so long as he doesn't set up full-time housekeeping with anyone.

6 / The Girls Say "Ah So!"

In bars and cabarets where hostesses get a percentage on the drinks they sell, the girls often over do it and become irritating in their efforts to get customers to spend more. So long as you continue buying drinks for yourself and them, they are very friendly and virutally anything goes. If you let too many minutes go by without buying another round, they will leave you the moment another customer comes in or as soon as they get bored with your company—and many of them get bored easily.

The most interesting explanation of this situation

I ever came across appeared recently in *Guide Plan Tokyo,* one of the several little guide books published in Tokyo for foreign visitors. The rundown was head-lined "Bright and Dim," and went:

"Now let's try an inquiry into the public resorts in Tokyo. But one word before you sail out into the sea of enjoyment lest sadness should steal upon the full tide of pleasure. You should be on your guard not to strike a rock of dubious house. There are, among the countless cabarets and night clubs, some mala fide holders. The charges, in general, are modest enough or, I might say, even much less than what you would be asked in New York or Paris, but what you must pay strict attention to is 'the drinks' brought for yourself and the hostess who might be just alone, might be two, three, or even more. The result can be what, at first, looked like a trifling expense of five or ten dollars amusement can easily become $20 or $30.

"What might embarrass you is the difficulty, due to the difference of language, in making yourself understood. Suppose you say, 'I have had enough. Must be leaving now,' they, upon your words, would laugh and say 'Ah, so' and order to bring more drinks. Of course, in most decent cabarets and night clubs, there are English speaking hostesses to attend you, dance with you, and make your evening enjoy-able. So, have fun now."

In every bar or club catering to foreigners there are always one or two girls who are outstanding in their ability to get customers to spend money. In

almost every case, these girls combine two characteristics: very large breasts and a lot of brains. The
best example I have seen of this type works in a
cabaret in Yokosuka that caters to American sailors.
This girl is about two inches taller than the average
Japanese girl, and has tremendous breasts. She wears
an especially low-cut gown that is designed to push
her breasts up high and reveal them down to the pink
of the nipples.

This young lady, who just reached seventeen,
keeps her eye on the door of the club and watches
especially for customers arriving in pairs or groups.
When a group comes in she immediately singles out
the ugliest lout in the lot, makes a beeline for him,
and then proceeds to give him the works, whispering
and blowing into his ear. Within thirty seconds after
they have sat down she has agreed to meet him after
she gets off work, and from then on he can't buy her
drinks fast enough.

In half an hour, she will have conned up to ten
drinks out of her victim; and often several for a girl
friend as well. As soon as she gets what she thinks
is the limit out of the poor slob, she starts watching
the door again and grabs the first new sucker that
arrives. By shifting from one table to another for
four or five minutes at a time, she is able to keep
several customers thinking that she is going to spend
the night with them.

When the fleet is in, this girl makes as much as
$100 a night; and according to several competing

girls, is still as pure of body as the day she was born.

Most bars or cabarets operating under this system have a special drink designed for the girls, and until recently it was often nothing more than colored water. So many of their foreign customers complained, however, that most now mix in enough alcohol to give the drinks a certain amount of kick.

Not all hostesses take advantage of this still watered down "special," though. Some, in fact, have become addicted to drinking themselves numb every night by matching their customers round for round. Several I have known over a period of years actually developed such a strong sense of fair-play that they insisted upon drinking what the customer drank to prove their sincerity.

A favorite technique, referred to rather hodge-podgedly by *Guide Plan Tokyo,* is for several hostesses, especially in higher-class bars and cabarets catering to Japanese clientele, to descend upon the newly arrived customer and all sit down with him. If the customer doesn't object immediately, he ends up having to buy drinks for a whole party, besides getting stuck with a hostess fee for every girl that got near him.

Greenhorns at the game can really get taken for a ride by this technique in the more unscrupulous places, where they are not above having every girl in the cabaret make like musical chairs.

Even knowing the system is no guarantee that you won't be taken. As soon as you step into many places you are immediately surrounded by a flock of girls who flutter around you like pretty butterflies, and it takes a man of very strong character—or absolutely no money—to drive them away before they get a chance to settle.

I recently stepped into a bar on the Ginza just to say hello to a friend of many years standing. During the few minutes I was there, my friend introduced me to four of her co-workers. When I left I was presented a bill for about $4, the cashier very correctly pointing out that I had taken up the time of five girls.

The primary reason for the existence of this system is that almost all Japanese customers of such places are authorized to spend company money and *want* to run up a large bill...in order to get back as much of a pre-arranged rebate as possible, or to keep their "slush" fund from being cut down because it wasn't all spent.

Many businessmen who are authorized to charge entertainment expenses to their company have a rebate arrangement set up with one or two places. When first starting the evening, they go to one of these places, run up a bill for several thousand yen and then tell the cashier to double or triple it and give them the difference in each. They then use this money to pay for drinking sprees in other bars, go to expensive restaurants, maintain mistresses, or visit hotspring resorts. Some of it may also be used for regular household expenses.

When a foreign customer enters such places, it seldom if ever occurs to the girls or management that he may *not* be on an expense account, or that he might be shocked at a bill for $30 when he only ordered $5 worth of drinks. On the contrary, they already take it for granted that all foreigners have money to throw away, and are very surprised when one so much as bothers to note how much a bill is.

This comes from the fact that traditionally the privileged class in Japan felt it degrading to discuss or be concerned with money or bills, and present-day tradesmen, who still automatically assume that no customer will ever question a bill, are very much taken back when one does.*

A significant percentage of the cabarets in Japan, in fact, take advantage of this very strong custom as part of their regular business policy, and their failure to consider that foreigners may not stand still for such conduct often gets them into trouble. Incidents in which some bar attempts to collect outrageous amounts from both Japanese and foreign customers are regular occurrences. One of the latest involved two visitors from Southeast Asia, who bought around $10 worth of drinks in a bar and were presented a bill for nearly $300 when they started to leave. The two Asians put up a fight, the police were called and the affair ended up as a minor

---

* Osakans, contrary to the general rule, are noted in Japan for being penny-pinching, hard-headed businessmen. If a customer in a Tokyo cabaret shows any interest in his bill he is often accused of being from Osaka.

international incident. Bars that go this far generally have several hoodlums on hand to force the customers to pay. So it is wise to avoid the more obvious dives.

About the only way to tell whether a place may be a dive or not is by the area that it is in and if there are any girls around. Bars that are potentially dangerous seem always to be found near pachinko parlors (a type of pinball machine), which are invariably in the hands of gangsters and generally have no girls around. Other signs to watch for include the appearance of the bar itself. If it is little more than a hole-in-the-wall without permanent-appearing facilities and decor, there is a good chance it may be dangerous.

Most such places are run by seasoned hoodlums, and are notorious for appearing overnight, systematically fleecing customers until it seems likely that the police are going to interfere, and then going out of business until things quiet down.

For the benefit of any ex-GI's who may have spent time in Japan several years ago and left with the idea that the young *chimpira* (punks) hanging around bars and pachinko parlors were not dangerous, times have changed. Several years ago it was true that even hardened hoodlums would go out of their way to avoid crossing a foreigner, and as a result many foreigners used to act like cocks of the walk.

Anyone who attempts such behavior nowadays is very likely to get a sword stuck in his stomach. When in Tokyo's Shinjuku area, particularly, revelers are cautioned to avoid provoking any of the several hundred punks infesting the various bar districts. They are now in the habit of making wisecracks and otherwise expressing their contempt when foreigners pass them in the narrow, dark streets. They are almost always in packs, and one or more will be armed.

To date, there have been only a few reported incidents of altercations between foreigners and Japanese hoodlums, but the potential danger of such incidents becoming commonplace is very great. There is a strong undercurrent of hate and contempt for the foreigner among a certain element of the Japanese. Some of this feeling has been carried over from the war and prewar days. Some of it, however, is being manufactured right now. One of the areas in which this is most noticeable is among young boys who are old enough to watch and understand television.

Several of my American friends whose bi-lingual children follow Japanese TV programs, report that their kids have been very subtly indoctrinated to dislike and look down on foreigners, and often come out with statements that are shocking.

So long as the bachelor confines his efforts to impressing the fairer sex, and exercises sensible caution in the choice of location, the likelihood of trouble in Japan is a great deal less, however, than what it is in many areas of the U. S. or France, for example.

FEW FOREIGN bachelors in Japan for any length of time have not had the experience of making arrangements to meet a cabaret girl after she gets off from work just before midnight, and having the girl not show up. Back in my own bachelor days in Tokyo, my friends and I were stood up regularly by girls who swore on sacred paper that they would keep their word and meet us. Yet we never gave up, and would stand on corners and in doorways for an hour before admitting that here was another girl who not only could resist our charms but had broken her solemn word.

After a number of years, some of us finally accepted the fact that a girl working in a cabaret catering to Japanese was not very likely to let herself become involved with or be seen in the company of a foreigner outside the cabaret. Most Japanese men resent the idea of Japanese girls associating with foreign men, and when the girls' livelihood depend upon the patronage of local customers, they naturally have to protect their own interest.

In addition to reserving their off-duty favors for Japanese patrons—if they go out at all with customers—a very large percentage of the girls working in

Japanese cabarets have steady boy friends who keep very close tabs on them. A significant number live with their boy friends.

The foreign bachelor who wants to develop a friendship with a girl working in this type of club will have better luck trying to set up a date on her day off. Or, as old pro's suggest, invite the cabaret girl to a late-night night club or a well-known restaurant after she gets off work.

Nearly every cabaret customer tries to date the hostesses. But the girls know that if they go out with a customer and stay overnight with him, chances are they will lose him as a customer. They also know that if they refuse a customer's overtures point-blank, they will also lose his patronage. So they become geniuses at keeping men in a state of suspended ecstasy.

The ideal situation, the girls say, is if they can successfully string a man along, sometimes for a period of several years, until they develop a true friendship. The customer will eventually stop trying to make out with them, but will continue being a good customer just the same.

I have often been on cabaret outings with Japanese friends who would introduce me to women they had been patronizing for thirty or more years.

The most dangerous part of the evening for cabaret girls is closing time when they have to somehow escape the waiting lotharios, or give in. A favorite ruse is for a girl to promise a man that she will let him take her home in his car or in a taxi. At the last moment, however, she invites several of her girl friends who live in the "same" direction to come along. Of course, would-be lover agrees to the extra passengers.

But the girls are in cahoots, and when there is only one "extra" girl to be dropped off, the intended victim comes up with some excuse to get out with her, leaving the customer nothing but a good Samaritan.

Cabaret-goers who have a rough time getting a cab on the Ginza or in Japan's other entertainment areas just before midnight, although the streets are full of taxis, are experiencing some of the effects of this "you can take me home" dodge. The taxi drivers are on the lookout for a single cabaret customer with three or four hostesses in tow. The driver knows the game the girls are playing, and knows the girls are likely to live in widely separated areas, and are therefore a profitable fare.

Another interesting custom probably unique to operators of Japan's "floating world" is the practice of arbitrarily raising their prices during the last few weeks of each year.

The pleasure purveyors argue that this is the season when regularly employed people get their year-end bonus, and they have a right to help themselves to a share.

They get by with this where Japanese customers are concerned for three reasons. In addition to being neurotically reluctant to say anything about the size of a bill presented to them by someone who expects to be paid on the spot, the Japanese (particularly Tokyoites) are fantastic spendthrifts when it comes to paying for entertainment.

Rather than try to *outfumble* each other when it comes to paying a bill in public places, Tokyoites *fight* for the right. On literally hundreds of occasions I have seen men engage in prolonged wrestling bouts over a check in name restaurants, knocking over chairs and upsetting dishes on tables.

This behavior stems from the inherent fear of the average Japanese of being out-done by someone in anything or put under obligation, and thereby insulted.

The third reason why the *mizu shobai* people can up their prices arbitrarily just before New Year's is because so many of their patrons are on company expense accounts, and could care less. They know that extra large bills at this time of the year are routine and will cause no unusual reaction in their company.

The receipts for money spent in bars, cabarets, and restaurants play an important role in the *mizu shobai*. In addition to turning in the ones that they acquire legitimately (that is by actually spending money to entertain customers), many people make a practice of "collecting" unclaimed receipts and including them in as part of their own expenditures ...pocketing this extra amount.

There are, in fact, professional collectors and buyers of unwanted receipts who sell them to company employees, usually for thirty to fifty per cent of their face value.

8 / An Orgy Of Night Life

THE SHEER volume of night life in Tokyo and other large cities in Japan is staggering. The number of bars, cabarets, semi-saloon coffee shops, party restaurants, party inns, and bathhouses in any of the major cities must be ten times more per capita than what exists in any comparable non-Japanese city in the world. The number of girls and women directly employed by these establishments in Tokyo alone is estimated to be well over half a million. There are approximately 150,000 cabaret hostesses alone.

Even more amazing than the number of "water businesses" in Japan, is the fact that most of them are bulging at the *benjo* (water-closet) with free-spending patrons nearly every night of the year. And there is a big difference between the drinking habits of the average Japanese Joe and his counterpart in the U.S. or Europe.

The average Japanese doesn't drop in at his favorite bar or cabaret for a couple of drinks and a bit of conversation before going home. He goes out for the whole evening to get drunk and have a loud, singing good time, usually hitting several places before the night is over.*

Reason for this preponderance of night life in Japan dates back from early times and is both economic and social.

From the first years of their history the Japanese were not thought of as individual units, but as parts of a group or clan, with the result that there was little or nothing personal in marriages and family raising. Japanese society therefore permitted men to engage in the pursuit of pleasure outside the home, including being as promiscuous as their financial means would allow.

A second social factor also contributed greatly to Japan's famous entertainment trades. Formal as well as informal Japanese life has always been so hedged in by such strict and fantastically complicated rules of etiquette that some kind of safety valve was needed to prevent neurotic explosions. This safety valve was provided by drinking. When a man was drinking he could laugh, cry, sing, dance, fight, curse, be sloppy, sentimental, lewd; in fact, do all the things that society denied him when he was sober.

Therefore, there was, and still is, a great compulsion for Japanese men to drink, and while drinking behave in an "un-Japanese" way. So strong is their desire for release from sober, "proper" behavior, that Japanese men can virtually will themselves drunk after drinking only a glass or two of beer or a few thimbles of *osaké*.

* This is known as *Hashigo-nomi* in Japanese; literally "ladder drinking." As used it refers to the fact that as a drinker goes from bar to bar he gets higher and higher.

There is still another reason why Japan's thousands of bars, cabarets, and related establishments are filled every night by a big percentage of the nation's adult male population. It is a relief from boredom. Their homes are small and very often shabby. They are hot and muggy during one part of the year and cold and damp during another. The food the common man eats at home is monotonous. Most Japanese are also so intellectually isolated and so tied to this monotonous routine of living that they must continuously fight to keep from being smothered by ennui. The ribald and raucous atmosphere of the "floating world" is their escape from dull reality.

This tremendous volume of night life in present-day Japan is made possible by a business system which makes large expense accounts and entertainment budgets available to managerial personnel down to a very low level, and in which hardly any business deal can be consummated without one or more visits to a Geisha house, cabaret, or party restaurant.

One of the routine tours favored by Japanese exporters entertaining their visiting buyers goes like this: (1) Begin at a very small, exclusive bar (well-patronized by the Japanese firm) for a few drinks and some suggestive banter with hostesses;

(2) Proceed to a *ryotei* (Japanese style restaurant) which has private rooms for each party, and there drink some more and eat as much as you can hold while being kept in the proper mood by friendly

waitresses who hover around each guest like harem girls;

(3) At about 10 p.m. some of the Japanese members of the party excuse themselves for an "important appointment" (usually a private date), then the diehards take the now tottering visitor to a large cabaret. Here comes dancing, flirting, provocative conversation, more drinking, and floor shows that range from classical Japanese dancing to stripping;

(4) Then if there is any sign that the buyer is still alive, he is taken to a Chinese restaurant and served a late night dinner that usually consists of a minimum of fifteen courses. He is also expected to drink like the rest of his life was going to be dry;

(5) Finally comes the last stop—a Turkish bath that features "special services."

If your Japanese host doesn't think this is enough to keep you as a steady buyer, he may drop a hint that if you would care to continue your own party...arrangements can be made so that you don't have to go to a dark hotel room all by yourself.

(The next morning at the office, the buyer will very likely be handed a bottle of *Guronsan,* a vitamin drink very popular in Japan for both hangovers and "sex-overs." The buyer will also be amazed at how bright and fresh his companions of the night before appear...and wonder how they can look forward to going through the same process again that night with another buyer.)

Although the nature of the *mizu shobai* is much

the same throughout Japan, there is sufficient difference in manners and attitudes in some areas to be
noticeable, even to a first-time visitor. Girls in Tokyo
tend to prefer a certain amount of ceremony and
make-believe in their relations with customers and
men friends. In Osaka, however, the girls are more
business-like and prefer to dispense with formalities.
Kyoto girls are generally considered the most charm-
ing and typically Japanese—except in the very commercial establishments where they are indistinguish-
able from their Tokyo sisters.

Girls and customs in the smaller prefectural cities
and towns differ primarily in the fact that they are
apt to be countryfied in speech and manners. Also,
the further you go out into the prefectures, the
stockier the girls tend to become. Many, it is true,
have beautiful faces when they are young, and pic-
tures of farm girls in colorful costumes that expose
only their face, are famous in Japan. But, in the buff
they present a very different picture.

The biggest problem in getting acquainted with
country girls, unless they are *mizu shobai,* is that they
are so shy and giggly that this in itself becomes an
almost impassable barrier. Very young girls, however, are often quite bold, and like nothing better
than to accost stray foreigners for the purpose of
practicing their school English. Unfortunately, they
lose this forwardness by the time they reach eighteen
or so.

Most of the services offered by Japan's cabarets

and bars are the old fashioned, traditional kind, but some are strictly space-age. Latest attraction featured in several of Tokyo's bars are oxygen inhalers for customers to sniff when they need pepping up.

The manufacturer of the new inhalers says a few sniffs a day gives the sniffer more energy, makes him feel younger, improves his appetite, and helps cure bronchial troubles.

Among the bars boasting bottled oxygen along with well-stacked hostesses, the best-known is the *Benizuru* (Red Crane) on the Ginza.

For the bachelor who might like to get pepped up at home on occasion, the inhalers are available from the maker at $139 each, including a mask, hose, and a two-foot long tank which holds sixty days supply of oxygen—at about 85 cents a tank.

(What with the dust, soot, car exhaust, and other filth that passes for air in Tokyo getting worse every day, the maker said he hoped to eventually install "oxygen boxes" on every street corner so passers-by can purchase a two-minute sniff for about two and a half cents.)

ONE OF the most popular pastimes and one of the largest "industries" in Japan is the custom of "Weekend Honeymoons" practiced by a sizable proportion of the population. Engaged in by both bachelors and married men, with girls and women from all classes and occupation, the custom consists of couples not married (to each other) going on weekend trips to one of hundreds of resort areas located throughout the country.

Many of the "Weekend Honeymooners" are young lovers who cannot or choose not to get married for some reason. Others are students out for a regular fling. A very large percentage are middle-aged businessmen out with a favorite cabaret girl or a young employee of some department of their company.

Some men take full advantage of this common practice to dally with a different girl each time, but the majority follow a more or less standard pattern of maintaining an alliance with the same girl for some months or longer, before a gradual breakup occurs, followed by a repetition of the same pattern with someone else.

Generally speaking, the older the man the longer the liasion can be expected to last. This happens because the older man, whose only attraction in the first place is his money, can afford to provide the girl with financial support on a regular basis.

The traditional idea that a man in Japan was not really a success until he could afford one or more mistresses is still very strong, and very much in evidence in such practices as weekend honeymoons.

Foreign visitors or residents in Japan are able to participate in this social sport to whatever degree they wish. A few keep track of passing time by the regularity of their sexual adventures, but most are not able to let themselves go beyond the occasional sortie.

Many men in Japan also take advantage of several peculiar "marriage" customs prevailing in the country. The one most often abused is "marrying" a girl but not legalizing it by failing to register the union at a government ward office.

A recent article in a local newspaper said the most striking instances of the injustices suffered by such common-law wives are found in those rural districts where the system of "trial marriages" is still practiced.

In farm families, the article continued, the new wife is considered simply as an addition to the family labor force. Through the "trial marriage," the family gets a chance to see whether a prospective wife lives up to expectations. These "marriages" are preceded by big receptions and celebrations. But the groom's family does not register the "wife" in the family register until she has successfully passed her "test."

This test period may last anywhere from six months to a year or more—being a matter that depends entirely on the whim of the "husband" or his parents. The girl has no say at all. After a year or so living with a man, a girl may be casually dismissed for such reasons as "she is not as hard working as we expected," "since she isn't pregnant yet, she is unlikely to have children," or even "she didn't have a sewing machine in her trousseau."

When such a "wife" is thrown out by her husband's family, she is entitled to neither alimony nor any other consideration. The separation is not regarded as a divorce because legally there never was a marriage.

In a Kyushu vilage, boys and girls must join the local Youth Association. During the charcoal-making season each year the boys and girls go up into the mountains and live together in huts "as husbands and wives." During the course of the season they trade partners at will so "pregancies seldom result." When a girl does become pregnant, however, and the father can be identified, the child is registered as his brother or sister—that is, the offspring of his parents.

In cities too, the article explains, there are social conditions which foster the practice of common-law marriages. Business companies are loath to keep married women on the payroll, and mariage usually spells the end of girl's employment. In order to get around this, some couples purposely do not register their marriage—thus allowing the wife to retain her single legal status.

For the same reason, co-eds who marry while still

at school do not register their marriages, in order to be able to get a job after graduation.

The most tragic cases are those of the day laborers who work on government relief projects. As such work is restricted to only one member per family, long-wedded couples often annul their marriages simply in order that both may work, continuing their hand-to-mouth existence as common-law husband and wife.

And there are still instances in today's advice-to-the-lovelorn columns of the situation that was a favorite tearjerker plot of cheap novels decades ago. The plot goes like this: a country boy leaves his fiance and comes to Tokyo to attend college. On a summer vacation at home, he "marries" her at a "private" wedding ceremony. They agree to postpone the official wedding and the signing of the marriage papers until the boy has graduated and found work.

Everything would be fine if this all happened as scheduled. But the boy may change his mind after three or four years at school because he finds a new girl friend, or, after he gets a job, he decides to marry the boss' daughter.

In the old pulp novels, the country girl was often depicted as returning home after a trip to Tokyo had shattered all her dreams of becoming her "husband's" legal wife.

But it is not only simple country girls who are enticed into such relationships. Many women who operate their own businesses are very susceptible.

They are usually in their thirties or forties and most of them are anxious to get married.

As the Japanese writer explained it: "With all their cleverness in business, these women often fall easy prey to soft-spoken wolves. They agree to set up housekeeping, with the hope that eventually the man will agree to legal marriage. But as soon as these male parasites have used up the women's savings, they say goodby and are off in search of another victim.

"Some of these women try to fight back, and take the case to a family court. But since they are common-law wives to begin with, they don't benefit much from such action. At most, they may receive some consolation money.

"The vague and ambiguous attitude often found in the Japanese character plays a part in creating common-law wives in this country. Some men don't bother to sign marriage papers simply because it is too much trouble. Others contend that love will take care of everything, and doubt the sincerity of women who want to go through the legal procedures necessary for an official marriage."

Social writers estimate that as high as forty per cent of the marriages in Japan are common-law.

DESPITE the imagination with which they have pursued sensual pleasure throughout their history, the Japanese never developed the art of kissing. In fact, up until the last few years it was considered a dirty, vulgar act engaged in only by gross barbarians.

By the middle 1950's, however, several hundred thousand American GI's and a steady diet of Hollywood's brand of adult sex had done what centuries of unbridled passion had been unable to do. At first the kissing one saw in movies and on television was rather passionateless and awkward. But there was nothing half-hearted about the way Japan's teenagers assimilated this new foreign import. Movie and TV film makers weren't long in gaining experience and following suit. Now some of the kissing scenes in Japanese movies begin where Hollywood leaves off.

In each of the country's major cities there are dozens of dark, cabaret-like saloons or bars which feature rows of single booths with high backs. From midmorning until after midnight, these booths are filled with couples who apparently never have to come up for air. Kissing in public is still rare in Japan, however, and foreign bachelors should be cautious about showing affection in this manner, particularly since their behavior is so conspicuous in the first place.

Dating is another Western custom which has found ready acceptance in Japan, but it is still in the early stages of development. In pre-1945 Japan, dating as Americans know it did not exist. Young men carried on with girls in redlight districts, and secret rendezvous in ryokan were common enough, but there was virtually no formal dating. About the only time any man appeared in public with a woman other than a Geisha or his mistress was at weddings and funerals. When in public with their husbands, women traditionally walked several paces behind.

By 1952, this centuries-old tradition had begun to crack, but it took the coming of age of the country's first postwar generation to shatter it once and for all. Influenced by foreign firms and the regular sight of GI's out with their girls, Japanese teenagers learned quickly and dating caught on.

By 1957, the country was alive with young couples who seemingly had appeared from nowhere in a matter of months. At first, they were self-conscious and never touched each other in public. But this is passing and it is no longer unusual to see a girl holding onto her boy friend's arm. They braver ones may walk with their arms around each other's waist.

This new development is also having its effect on married couples of all ages. Many now take weekend trips together and visit restaurants and theaters, often without their children.

11 / Boy Hunts & Girl Hunts

IN OLD Japan the social system prevented young people from associating freely with each other, and it was difficult for them to have a circle of friends among the opposite sex. Today's teenagers are well on the way toward a final solution of this problem, however, and the more successful they are the easier it becomes for foreign bachelors. Their solution is just as simple as it is direct. They go on boyfriend or girlfriend hunts, whichever the case may be; and there surely is no clearer sign of how rapidly Japan's old feudalistic society is breaking up.

These forays of friend-hunting by young men and girls are not haphazard or casual affairs. They are serious efforts that are formally recognized and labeled *boi hanto* (boy hunt) and *garu hanto* (girl hunt)—and sometimes "man hunt"; all terms taken intact or adapted from recent American movies.

The leaders of this new movement are Japan's several hundred thousand high school and college students, among a great many of whom sex has become a sport on a par with baseball and mountain climbing.

According to a recent poll, the biggest problem facing young Japanese girls today, however, is still meeting the "right man." Approximately 51 per cent of the girls polled said they knew they had little chance of marrying if they waited for the "right man" to come along. As a result, these girls were prepared to accept an arranged marriage. The remaining 49 per cent said they wanted a "love marriage" or nothing. Sixty-seven per cent of the girls said they thought virginity was an important asset to a would-be bride. According to the weekly magazine *Manga Tengoku* (Comic Heaven), however, only one out of three unmarried Japanese girls is a virgin!

The survey found that young girls in their early teens were more apt to have boyfriends than older girls. It was estimated that one-fifth of the million and a half girls in Tokyo who are between the ages of 15 and 24 have never had a boyfriend or date. It was also discovered that the typical boyfriendless girl lived with her parents, and if she was over 20 was apt to be a nurse or a teacher.

To the modern Japanese girl, personality in a male is more important than love, looks, or income. Seventeen per cent of the girls surveyed were outspoken in their attitudes toward premarital sex relations. They said they saw nothing morally or socially wrong with the practice as long as they liked the men concerned.

Of course, bachelor men have their problems too. Single men working for Yawata Iron & Steel company recently planned a dance. Because none of them had girlfriends they placed an advertisement in a local newspaper asking girls to attend. The results were overwhelming. Special arrangements had to be made to take care of all the girls who showed up.

Despite the tremendous changes that have taken place, the foreign bachelor in Japan still cannot operate like he would in the United States or some European country. First of all, nearly all Japanese parents are strongly opposed to the idea of their daughters associating with foreigners. This feeling is both racial and nationalistic.

There is also a traditional, deep-seated feeling among the average Japanese that any Japanese girl who associates with a foreign man is no better than a prostitute, regardless of the circumstances. Young men, especially, are prone to look upon each separate case as a personal as well as national insult.

Secondly, the language barrier and differences in social customs restrict the areas in which foreign bachelors can meet and get acquainted with Japanese girls. Dances, private house parties and other such occasions at which young men meet eligible girls in Western countries, are still exceedingly rare in Japan.

Even at this late date, so sensitive is the relationship between men and women that it is commonly accepted by young Japanese girls that a man, especially a foreigner, has more than a platonic interest when he asks for their name and address.

This can be very embarrassing to the girl concerned. If she and her family, or friends who know of the approach, happen to be "old fashioned," her reputation will be permanently tainted.

As a result, most foreign-Japanese girl relationships

begin in the "floating world"; in bars, cabarets, and night clubs, where the girls are already outside the pale of respectable society. The first date with a girl from the *mizu shobai,* more often than not, ends up as an all night affair at some hotel if the man wants it that way.

Coffee shops are now said to be the biggest pickup places for young Japanese, and surprisingly perhaps, girls and women often take the initiative in making the first move. Those in the know say it is more or less an unwritten rule that a girl who takes more than 10 minutes to pick up a date doesn't make the grade. Among the coffee shop crowd sexual relations are referred to as *esu* ("S") *no kankei* (sex relations), or *Namba shikkusu no kankei* (No. 6 relations) "because sex gives them such a wonderful feeling it takes six senses to enjoy it fully".

Many coffee shops stay open all night by serving food with every order after 11 P.M., since restaurants do not come under the 11 o'clock curfew law. Some put up a sign saying, "Pay Waiting Room," then charge about 35 cents for a face towel and a cup of tea, and claim they stay open for husbands and wives who work in the evening and need some place to meet afterward.

House parties are becoming the rage among well-to-do high school age boys and girls who attend private schools—and therefore don't have to study as hard as those in public schools. The parties are held in the students' homes when their parents are away for the day or night. Participants share the cost of food and drinks. At the typical party the *patisutos* (partyists), as they are called in Japanese, dance the latest dances, gradually working themselves into frenzies during which they shout and scream. Some of the parties last all night and are a little more serious, the *patisutos* getting high on drinks or pills, pairing off and taking rooms or going to nearby love inns.

12 / Cars As Bachelor Accessories

AUTOMOBILES, the boudoir of young America, are growing in importance in Japan as social accessories. At this stage, only the upper-middle class and above can afford to own a car privately, but large numbers of other people use company-owned vehicles for private purposes.

In Tokyo alone there are some 100,000 small delivery trucks, most of which are used by their owners or drivers for private transportation, and it is now common to see young couples as well as whole families stuffed into a little 3-wheeler out visiting or on a Sunday drive.

When a young man in Japan can afford (or borrow) a car to take his girl friend out, they sit close together, just like in American movies. Until the early 1960's there was little necking or petting in cars, since there are few sanctions against couples check-ing into an inn if they want to play; but times have changed.

At beaches during the summer time, especially, couples in their teens have discovered that cars can be used for more than transportation. Still, the future of cars as accessories for bachelors in Japan appears to be slim. Where visiting foreign bachelors are con-cerned it is dark indeed.

Roads and streets in Japan are horribly inade-quate. In Tokyo and other major cities the traffic problem is so bad, despite new free-ways and other improvements forced through before and after the 1964 Olympics, that owning and operating a car is a frustrating and dangerous business.

At one stage of its development, for example, the area that is now known as Tokyo officially consisted of 808 different little towns clustered around and on seven low hills.

Over the decades, these little towns grew until their boundaries overlapped. Then sometime in the late 1600's people started calling this conglomeration a city. There was no special effort to integrate these tiny townships into a unified whole. Each retained its own system of completely haphazard alleys and foot paths.

Present-day Tokyo has managed to perpetuate the character and physical appearance of its early years, with the result that it is the world's largest labyrinth.

Out of the original 808 towns, around fifty have

grown into sizable cities in their own right, but most of the others remain sandwiched in between train stations and better-known areas, their history all but forgotten.

The roadways within these areas, except for certain small districts in the major ones, are still as narrow, as rough and as haphazard as they were two hundred years ago. To add to the interest, less than one per cent of the "streets" in Tokyo are named, and no address of any building or house has any connection with any street it may be on or near.*

Tokyo proper is divided into 23 wards. Each of these wards is divided into an indefinite number of *machi* and or *cho,* both of which mean "town" (and more or less represent the hundreds of little towns of Old Tokyo). These areas are further divided into *banchi* (lot-numbers), which are often translated as "blocks." This is misleading, however, since *banchi* are anything but square and have no standard size.

Addresses therefore go like this: Tokyo, the name of the Ward, the name of the *machi* and/or the number of the *cho* (there may be both), the *banchi,* which represents the house number, and finally the

* The only practical, systematic effort that has ever been made to help foreigners get around in Tokyo without an interpreter-guide, is my own self-guider or taxi guide to Tokyo. In the form of a shirt-pocket sized booklet, the *De Mente Taxi Guide To Tokyo* consists of selected places pinpointed by location maps oriented in Japanese. All the visitor has to do is show the proper listing to a taxi driver, and at worst he will get you within fifty feet of your destination. The self-guide is available at leading hotel bookshops in Japan, and at many leading bookstores in the U.S. and other countries.

name of the building or person. There are usually several buildings or persons with exactly the same address, so once you get down to *banchi,* the only way to locate the place you want is by elimination.

This, as you can imagine, causes visiting foreigners considerable trouble, and results in most of them confining their travel in Tokyo to guided tours, the immediate area around their hotel, and the Ginza shopping district—which is one of the half a dozen or so small areas in Tokyo that has fairly straight streets blocked at regular angles.

Despite this obstacle, many foreign residents still prefer to own a car (and a few of the bachelor-types have truly fantastic stories to tell about their back-seat successes), but short-term visitors are better off sticking to trains for longer trips (anything outside of Tokyo, etc.) and the ubiquitious taxi for shorter, mad dashes within cities.

The only exception might be renting a car for a weekend trip into the mountains or country-side. Even then it is foolish for the average foreigner to go without a driver-guide if he doesn't know where he is going and doesn't speak Japanese.

13 / In Japan You're Never Too Old!

ONE OF the most noteworthy characteristics of Japanese girls is that they have fewer qualms about associating with elderly men than their Western counterparts. The reason for this is both social and economic. Girls in Japan have traditionally been educated and conditioned to accept the idea of fraternizing with older men; and young men couldn't afford the expenses involved. This resulted in Japan becoming a paradise for older men.

While the economic situation of young men has improved considerably in the last few years, and they now participate in the great game of pleasure on more equal terms with their fathers, the old man in Japan enjoys privileges and opportunities that men in other countries can only dream about.

The most interesting demonstration of this situation that I recall seeing occurred in Atami before Japan's redlight districts had their licenses withdrawn. I was sitting on a canal-side bench that commanded a good view of one of the city's main redlight districts, just after the houses opened for business on a Sunday afternoon.

Shortly after I took up this position, a baldheaded, toothless old man that must have been near 80, shuffled by me in wooden clogs and yukata robe, and headed down into the redlight area.

Each side of the street was lined with girls who

began calling to the old man. Some of them changed their standard pitch from "O'ni-san, agarimasen ka?" (which means something like, "How about coming up—or climbing on—big brother") to "How about climbing on, grand-dad?"

The girls were laughing and enjoying themselves but the old man looked neither right nor left, and was very careful to stay in the exact center of the street where he couldn't be reached by clutching hands.

Just as he came even with about the fourth house down, however, four girls suddenly dashed out of a doorway and pounced on him. Two of the girls grabbed his legs and the other two his arms, and while he kicked and screamed for the police, the four carried him bodily into their house.*

His protests had been loud and apparently sincere, so I expected him to reappear as soon as the house madame saw and heard what was going on, but he didn't, and within seconds everything was back to normal.

---

* Many redlight district girls who realized that their face wasn't pretty enough to attract customers often resorted to clever stategems to make up for this weakness. The one I thought was best of all was worked by a girl on the cheap side of Shinjuku 2-chome in Tokyo. The front of the house in which this girl worked was all shadowed except for a foot-wide streak chest-high across the door. Whenever a potential customer came abreast of the door, the girl would suddenly step into this natural spotlight and pull her sweater down from the top, exposing the largest pair of *chichi* I have ever seen on a Japanese girl. This usually stopped whoever was passing as if they had hit a wall. After about three tantalizing seconds, the girl would then step back into the black maw of the door, drawing the more susceptible men in after her like they were on a leash.

I waited and watched the doorway of the house into which he had disappeared. About twenty minutes later he stepped out, as brisk and peppy as you please and wearing a grin that split his face in two.

This phenomena of older men enjoying themselves with younger girls is most obvious in Japan's many cabarets, where some ninety per cent of the regular patrons are over thirty, and at least half are over forty.

One recent American visitor who wouldn't rate a smirk from any woman under forty in the U.S., was in a state of stunned ecstasy at the treatment he received from girls in Tokyo. In trying to explain what it was like, he could only sigh and say, "I didn't know it could be so good!"

I don't know how much scientific evidence there might be to support such a contention, but for all practical purposes, the *mizu shobai* girls in Japan are the closest you can get to discovering the fountain of youth.

Put a man of sixty into a crowd of seductive-looking and provocative-mannered girls in their teens and twenties, with the full knowledge that they are available, that society approves, that most if not all of the girls are willing (they all act eager enough), and he'd have to be dead or a deviate not to react.

14 / The Free-Lovers

In Japan's large cities there is a class of girls who are essentially sensualist-minded in their outlook on life, and the bachelor who gets into this circle has his work cut out for him. These girls, who generally are around 17 to 19 years old (but sometimes come as young as 14), are most numerous in the many art schools that flourish in Tokyo, Osaka, and similar cities. They are also frequently found in bars, cabarets, and coffee shops.

By the nature of their interest, they are already non-conformists, and this is accompanied by an avid interest in experiencing as much life as they can in the shortest possible time. To most, this means simply sexual pleasure in all its ramifications.

Girls of this type that work in bars are prone to be moody and heavy drinkers, and during their moody periods, tend to talk about being tired of life and thinking about killing themselves. They are gay, in a cynical way, and very daring when drinking.

The other half of this group, the arty-type, are far more interesting. They are serious in their pursuit of experience and emotion, and go about it with singular dedication and, after a short time, considerable skill. As in the case with most Japanese intellectuals, these girls also go through a foreign phase in which they try to extend their research to foreigners. Those who succeed in making the first foreign contact generally find their new-found friend more than glad to help them widen their range.

Among the girls of this type that I have known, one was especially interesting. I first meet her when she was sixteen, and still in school. Her ambition, she very proudly pointed out when she was about seventeen, was to have an affair with a man of every race and nationality. Her favorite hunting ground was the Foreign Correspondent's Club in Tokyo.

By the time she was nineteen, she had exhausted all the more common nationalities—going through some in depth—and had gotten tired of waiting for the uncommon ones to show up. The last time I talked with her, she was pretty well frustrated and was looking for an opportunity to travel abroad.

While it would be dangerous to attempt to identify such girls by a physical description alone, they do seem to share common physical as well as mental characteristics that distinguish them from the crowd. Most important is that they mature younger and better, and seem to radiate a sensuality that is animal-like in its intensity. They also seem to prefer flats to heels, and wear little or no make-up.

TURKISH bathhouses in Japan today are not the open sex palaces of the early days of *Yedo*, but many are luxurious in a gaudy way. Scantily clad young girls still dispense various grades of "service" in imitation of their famed predecessors, and the trend is for more, bigger, and flashier bathhouses to replace (as they did once before) the outlawed redlight districts.

In the last few years, dozens of new baths have sprung up in Tokyo and other cities (at the last count, there were some 200 in Tokyo), and there is every reason to predict that more will follow. The larger ones usually include a restaurant and one or more bars or cabarets on the same premises. They also provide catering service for patrons while they are being bathed and administered to.

The routine for ordinary patrons is simple. They are ushered into a small private room containing a bunk-like massage bed, a clothing rack or closet, a wall mirror, and usually one or two pieces of furniture. In an adjoining room will be a bath and sweatbox. (Some of the larger houses have giant public baths accommodating up to a hundred bathers at a time. The sexes are segregated in these non-private baths, but there are usually girl masseuses in the men's section.)

A girl—in some bathhouses there may be two girls—dressed in brief shorts and bra greets the guest, helps him undress, gives him a small towel to wrap around his waist if he desires, and then locks him up in the sweatbox.

When the customer indicates that he has sweated enough, the girl lets him out, has him soak for a couple of minutes in a tub of hot water, and then proceeds to wash him down while he sits on a stool. Just when the uninitiated guest thinks he is going to get something for nothing, the girl hands him the soap, and points to his privates.

(Bachelor informants who prefer to remain anonymous tell me that this is now strictly true only at *Tokyo Onsen* on the Ginza, where most foreign visitors are taken. They say that at other bathhouses, the girls do their duty.)

The sweating and bathing generally take up about thirty minutes, then the guest is led to the massage bunk and told to lie down on his stomach. If there are two girls they divide the body up and work on different parts. Most have little or no professional knowledge of massaging, and simply squeeze, pull, thump and pound like old-time mattress-softners. But it is relaxing and grows on one.

While the beating you get from two girls is better than what you get from one, it is less interesting unless you happen to speak Japanese, because the girls usually keep up a constant stream of chatter between themselves and hardly ever look at the guy they are working on.

The cost of this type of service varies from the

equivalent of around $3 to $5 for an hour to seventy-five minutes, depending on the bathhouse; plus a tip of fifty cents or so for each girl.

At this type of session, there is usually a bit of suggestive horseplay, and certainly enough play of the imagination to make most visitors feel like they are getting their money's worth.

This is what happens to the uninitiated. Those in the know have a choice if they want to exercise it. There are a few bathhouses where no hanky panky is allowed, and there are times when police pressure forces other houses to keep clean* for indefinite periods. But most of the time in most of them, all the guest has to do is make his real intentions clearly known immediately upon being ushered into the private room, *not after bathing*.

The un-informed invariably wait until they are on the massage bunk to make their play, without any effort to settle the business side of it first, and in most instances are turned down flat.

Simply because most foreigners can't read Japanese, they miss out on one of the popular standard services (offered by most if not all Turkish bathhouses in Japan) that is generally not available elsewhere under similar circumstances.

This service, which is announced in Japanese along with other services on a framed plaque hanging on the wall of the bathhouse rooms, is advertised as a "Hormone Massage" and consists of "Miss Turkish

* pun.

Bath" masturbating the guest. This type of massage, the English-language brochures say, "serves as a solvent of what is called 'stress' disease."

The brochures further state: "Why don't you drop in so that you may long remember your happy days in Japan. We are all ready to serve you with the tenderest, and most satisfying service possible."

Of course, people who don't care for this type of service don't have to accept it. They should keep in mind, however, that it is a practice that has stood the test of time, and is highly recommended by all honest doctors and psychologists familiar with the nature of man.

Members of the Diner's Club may use their credit cards at some of Japan's bathhouses.

Just before the Tokyo Olympics in the fall of 1964 several Japanese women's organizations and a number of female Diet members made a determined effort to have the activities of the flourishing Turkish bath houses curbed. Eventually they were able to get regulations passed which made it illegal for the bath girls to minister to customers in private behind locked rooms while dressed in shorts and halters. Bath house operators were instructed to see that their girls wore robes, that all doors remained unlocked and that all rooms were provided with peep-hole windows so activity in the rooms could be seen from the outside. When this bombshell hit the bath house fraternity it was wildly predicted that there would be a sharp decline in the number of customers, and that the popular bath houses would soon disappear.

Fortunately for the men in Japan (and the girls who enjoy the well-paying profession) things did not work out quite like the women crusaders intended. Enforcing such regulations under the free enterprise system now prevailing in Japan was simply impossible. As usual, members of the Turkish Bath House Association met, deplored the action of the Government and then passed their own set of regulations which were even more binding than those passed by the Government. Of course, this latter action was just a smoke screen and none of the regulations were carried out.

The controversy has not died down altogether. Both the police and the press regularly "investigate" the bath house situation. The police discover over and over again that most of the bath house girls offer any kind of "service" customers want, but they cannot prove anything against the house operators. The press takes a rhetorical view. A recent story observed that if a naked man is locked in a private room with a scantily clad girl who bathes and massages him, some reaction should be expected. The story went on: "Most of the customers have been drinking, but they are generally rather quiet so it is often said they come along with a secret intention. When one enters a Turkish bath house a receptionist asks him: 'Do you have a *shimei* (a regular girl)?' If the customer does not request a specific girl the receptionist rings a bell and which ever free girl is first in line comes out wearing a gown over her shorts and bra. After greeting the customer she leads him to her room. The customer and the girl are soon on intimate terms. When the girl washes his feet or some other part, the customer seeks a chance to put his hand in her bra or nip her hips. Most of those who do such mischief are said to be middle-aged gentlemen. The girl will warn, 'You shouldn't do such a thing!' But the man does not stop. Finally the girl threatens to scream or call for help. Then the man says, 'Things are rather dull. It is not as much fun as I expected. How much do you charge for the special service?' "*

Following the Tokyo Olympic Games a *mizu shobai* authority noted: "Before the Games Turkish baths were taken up by the Diet as a problem that insults the national prestige, but the baths should be considered as places where love affairs are readily available. 'Weren't the activities of the Turkish baths restricted during the Games?' you will ask. On the contrary, not only were they continued but they contributed more to the promotion of international goodwill than any other thing!"

In current *mizu shobai* parlance, a "full course" at a Turkish bath consists of a steam bath, being washed and massaged by the bath girl, and then being offered "special" or "double" service. Explains

---

* The term "special service" used to be rather general and referred to all the more common sexual practices. Now it usually refers to oral-genital contact only.

a popular weekly magazine: "In the past, 'special service' generally referred to the bath girl masturbating the guest by hand. Now it refers to using the mouth and has recently come to the point where the customer's whole body is 'served' by the lips of the bath-girl. 'Double service' refers to oral-genital contact followed by *honban* ("the real thing," i.e. coitus). The rates for full course service at a bath house in Ikebukuro are about $3 for the bath, an additional $6 for 'special service' and another $9 for *honban*.

There is nothing new about the so-called "special service" offered by bathhouse girls. It has long been a common practice in Japan. But it has been much in the news lately because it is being exploited as a substitute for prostitution, which has been forced underground.

The latest "special service" story to be made public in Japan caused something of a flap at the Foreign Office. Word got back to Tokyo that a Japanese authoress who has become well-known by writing detailed descriptions of her own sexual experiences is "researching" her way through the U.S. and Europe by "special servicing" prominent men she meets on her travels, then writing up the experiences for publication back home. According to a magazine write-up of the travels and triumphs of Miss X, she also engages in regular intercourse for the sake of material, but finds the special Turkish Bath service is much more convenient because neither party has to disrobe or lie down and because it can be accomplished in a matter of a minute or two in almost any location.

Every once in a while the police raid 30 to 40 of the bathhouses and arrest the owners and managers, but they cannot close the places down. According to the Tokyo Metropolitan Police Department, 70 to 80 per cent of the bathhouses in the city are owned or controlled by gangsters. Other gangsters specialize in supplying the houses with runaway girls, as well as squeezing money out of girls whom they have made their lovers.

Bachelors in Osaka shouldn't miss the New Japan in the Dotombori entertainment district. It is the world's largest, consisting of eight floors above ground and two below. There is a special woman's bath on the fourth floor, a giant man's bath (non-private) on the fifth floor, and a garden bath that accommodates one hundred on the seventh floor. The first and second floors are taken up by a cabaret. Private baths account for the remaining floors.

No matter what you go for, the baths are interesting and well worth the fee. They are especially convenient during the muggy, dirty months of mid-summer when you get all sweated up during the day and don't want to go home or back to your hotel to clean up. Local businessmen who have a bad case of hangover often slip out and spend an hour in a nearby bath.

Japan's Turkish baths also cater to couples who want to bathe together. When such couples want to dispense with the services of the bath girls, and have the private room all to themselves, they tip the girl (or girls) and tell her to take the hour off—which she is very glad to do.

16 / Maids In Ryokan Are Taboo

MANY newcomers to Japan automatically assume that maids employed in the numerous ryokan, especially those in the resort areas catering to unmarried couples, are included in the establishment's services.

While there are exceptions, generally this is not true in the ryokan approved by the Japan Travel Bureau or Japan Tourist Association for foreign visitors.

Among the few isolated cases in which it was reported that a maid paid a nocturnal visit to a traveler's room in an "approved" ryokan, one stands out.

In this case, the traveler reports that three maids were assigned to take care of him—prepare his bath, serve his meals and lay out the sleeping mats at bedtime. One was quite pretty, one was fair, and the third was a witch. As most men will, the traveler acted friendly and interested in all of them without seriously expecting anything to come of it.

But after he had been in bed for some time and had already fallen asleep, he was awakened by someone who crawled in with him and very quickly demonstrated her intentions. The interlude was over before. he realized he didn't know which one of the girls had visited him, and he left the inn the next day without finding out. Ordinarily, if a bachelor wants to play games in this type of inn, he has to provide his own equipment.

In most of southern Japan, however, particularly in Kyushu, there is a type of inn where female companionship is the main course on the bill, and is offered to all comers.

17 / Nude-Viewing As A Pastime

JAPAN offers opportunities for nude-viewing not generally existing in other countries, and the pleasant part is that this interesting hobby can be engaged in more or less openly and without fear of jeopardizing your reputation—although it might have an adverse affect on your subsequent social successes.

The main arena for nude-viewing in Japan are the thousands of baths in which mixed bathing, for everyone who prefers it, is still the rule. Most of these baths are part of the facilities of inns in hot-spring resort areas, which abound all over Japan.

In a predictably reactionary move, the Japanese are beginning to re-emphasize traditional customs and pleasures such as mixed bathing. Right after the Pacific war and for several years thereafter mixed bathing was looked upon by the more Westernized Japanese as an undesirable appendage of their "uncivilized past". Now it is coming back into favor. "Co-baths" are being used by many resort hotels to attract customers. One of the most spectacular of these new co-baths is one at Tadami-machi in Hiroshima Prefecture. It is located in a large cave.

Many foreign visitors to Japan are hesitant about participating in this traditional custom, but there is really nothing to it once you get the hang of it. The main idea is just to pretend that you are used to parading around in the nude in front of a bunch of people, and be nonchalant about the whole affair.

(Squeemish people are allowed to hold a small hand-towel in front of them, but no real man would stoop that low.)

You might also keep in mind that the Japanese are taught to ignore nudity when it occurs in a prescribed manner in established places, like the bath, the toilet, aboard trains, and in the streets.

So long as you, in turn, don't stare at your fellow bathers, you can get quite an eyefull. Of course, this requires a special technique, sort of like a glassy-eyed panning with a camera, but with a little practice you'd be surprised at how much detail you can take in. This exercise also helps you develop a really amazing peripheral vision.

One of the most interesting experiences I have encountered in this field occurred in an isolated farming community in Gumma Prefecture some time ago.

On the night that I happened to be visiting a certain farmer, it was his turn to run a bath and invite his neighbors in to use it.

Since the farm house, like most, was very practically constructed, with the kitchen, bath, and dining room (where we spent the evening) all in one large split-level room, the neighbors using the bath were in full view of everyone else in the room.

As it happened (I was told it was because they wanted to see the foreigner), all the young girls in the neighborhood came in to take a bath, and my host took great delight in introducing me to each of them while they were going about their bathing. The thought kept occurring to me: "What a fine way to introduce a bachelor to the eligible young ladies of a community!" Probably still a little advanced for most American communities, however.

A second and more sensational area of nude-viewing in Japan are the many nude art studios, some of which cater to foreigners. (One of the interesting facets of the nature of Japanese men is that although they have grown up in the midst of nudity, so to speak, they are still attracted by the idea of a surreptitious visit to a nude studio.)

While there are some exceptions, most of the nude studios are just that, and only a genuine camera addict would appreciate them. Most are located in run-down, cruddy buildings, and the attendants generally look like gangsters or dope fiends, although every so often you run into the long-haired arty type.

Models in the nude studios range from farm girls who have run away to the big city and strippers who can't get booked anymore, to students who are out earning pin money.

On occasion, especially among girls from this latter group, there will be one that is outstanding. But on the average, they're about as rundown as the building the studio is in. Those that street touts work with are generally the lowest in the class.

The only bit of equipment necessary to gain admittance to a nude studio is a camera. Some studios will allow a group to go in when only one of them has a camera. Everyone has to pay a fee, however. And charges run from about $1.50 to $6 or so per thirty minutes.

Several of the studios in Tokyo that are "exceptions" offer quite a bit more than undraped girls climbing around on black studio pads. Girls from these places are allowed to accompany the customer for "location" shots. A number of these studios advertise regularly in the classified ad section of the English language *Mainichi Daily News.* Some of them will send a car to pick you up at your hotel.

Another form of entertainment that flourished during the heyday of the Occupation and is now experiencing a revival, are the so-called "private shows," which consist of live demonstrations of an intimate nature.

Touts hang out around downtown stations, burlesque theaters, and drinking areas, and accost passing foreigners in the grandest Hollywood tradition.

The most popular "private show" is said to be a situation in which one or more girls invite an unsuspecting man into what appears to be a private room but is actually fixed up with eye holes or a one-way mirror so that a small audience can watch everything that takes place. The girls are paid performers playing a part, and naturally see that the "star" puts on a good show. In Tokyo, most of these shows are staged in the Asakusa district.

18 / Action On The Beach

THERE are a number of things at which the Japanese qualify as fanatics. One of these is going to the beach. During the months of July and August it is often hard to get near the water in such popular seaside areas as Kamakura and Enoshima, both of which are about an hour's train ride from Tokyo.

This situation has its compensations, however, in that such tremendous gatherings of people in a holiday mood offer the bachelor many rare opportunities.

Japanese beaches are especially interesting because of distinctive attitudes the people have about changing clothes and going into the water. Since clothes-changing and bathing are natural bodily functions, it has always been natural for the Japanese to engage in these actions openly. The idea of hiding themselves would have struck them as both funny and curious until a few years ago.

The Western concept of prudery is growing rapidly in Japan, but enough commonsense still prevails to provide a contrast. A few years ago, Japan's beaches were one giant, continuous strip show, as people changed from street clothing to swim wear and back again without doing much more than turning their backs. Women often would lay an umbrella down and step behind it, but this blocked the view from only one side.

Swim wear during this period also contributed to the sights to be seen on Japan's beaches. The average girl's one-piece wool bathing suit was made like a man's undershirt at the top and a pair of jockey shorts at the bottom. In addition to barely covering the essentials when dry, the suits were a farce when wet. Each time the wearer came out of the water or was hit by a wave, the upper part of the suit collapsed down to around her waist.

Current Japanese-made swim wear has improved to the point where it isn't as interesting as it used to be—except that designer-makers haven't gotten around to noticing that proportion-wise it generally takes more material to cover a woman's bottom than it does a man's. (Informants who should know, say that this is actually done on purpose—to make the stubby legs of most Japanese girls look longer.)

Primary interest now is provided by the crowds of

girls who come to the beaches for excitement. Many are ordinary office and school girls down for a day or weekend, but hundreds come from well-to-do families and spend most of the summer on the beach. Best time for making contact is from dusk until about 10 p.m. Techniques include using a beach ball to get a little group game going (if a prospect looks friendly, make play-ball motions) and renting one of the large rubber life boats available all along the beaches, and enticing the girls aboard.

A word of warning: Japan's beaches also attract racketeers and thugs who prey on couples and others who stray away from the crowded areas or stay out after most everyone else has called it a day. The problem is serious enough that several squads of police patrol the beach areas in pairs, but they can't watch everyone.

Bachelors operating in the dark should take care that both flank and rear are well guarded.

Prosperity has also opened up another hunting ground for the bachelor in Tokyo during the summer months. It is now fashionable for movie stars, models and, recently, high-income cabaret girls, to spend several afternoons a week at the Akasaka and Shinagawa Prince Hotel swimming pools.

Since acquaintances are easier to strike up in a pool-side atmosphere, it wasn't long before the word spread and the city's eligible men began to take advantage of the situation.

A number of bachelor friends report they have

had excellent success in meeting these girls by going to the pools during lunch hours and the early afternoon. If your physique is not one of your strong points, however, it might be best not to parade it in the bright light.

19 / Fertility Festival Anyone?

THE CORE of Shinto belief, Japan's native "religion," is the idea of fertility, and this, from earliest times, has been primarily manifested by the worship of phallic symbols, particularly the male organ.

This worship has traditionally taken two forms—the erection of phallic symbols at road intersections and other auspicious places, and the staging of annual fertility festivals revolving around life-like reproductions's of the male *chimbo,* ranging from watch-fob to Paul Bunyan-size.

In present-day Japan, these fertility festivals have survived in such areas as Aichi, Shizuoka, Fukuoka, and Kumamoto prefectures, and afford the visitor a rare opportunity to see a side of Japan that dates from pre-historic times. The grand finale of the festival held in Kumamoto is very impressive. A gang of young men carry (or pull on a wagon) through the streets a full-color reproduction of a man's penis carved out of a log that measures up to thirty feet in length and is about two feet in diameter.

The Japan Travel Bureau at one time had an excellent technicolor documentary film of a similar festival, but knowing that foreigners generally prefer to confine their public celebrations to pumpkins and may-poles, were careful about whom they showed it to.

Bachelors might find it interesting to take their own films of this colorful festival. It might come in handy on one of those long evenings when you run out of something to talk about.

Most convenient of the fertility festivals for visitors to take in is the one staged on the 15th of every month by the *Tagata Jinja* (Tagata Shrine) in Aichi Prefecture's Komaki City near Nagoya. Once a year, on March 15th, this shrine holds a Grand Festival.

On regular monthly festival days, priests of the shrine sell phallic symbols to worshippers and interested visitors. Part of the festival consists of women carrying horse-sized *chimbo* from one place to another.

Chimbo sold to worshippers and visitors vary in size and type. Some are made of ceramic (Aichi Prefecture is the center of Japan's chinaware industry) and some are made of wood. Types range from normal-sized replicas in various colors to miniature ones designed to be carried in a woman's purse or worn as accessories.

Biggest buyers of the blessed *chimbo* are women who want to become pregnant.

About a mile down the road from the Tagata

Shrine is a *Jinja* for women, where all the phalli are female.

A fertility rite still practiced in Oguchi City, Kagoshima Prefecture (Kyushu) is known as *Harame,* which is a command meaning "Become pregnant!"

In this rite, children under seven years of age go around to the homes of childless couples on January 7th, call the wife out, and while poking her stomach with phallic-shaped roots, shout: "Get pregnant! Get pregnant! Kick the bride out if she can't get pregnant!"

If the wife does not come out and submit to this ceremony, the parents of the children, who have been trailing along behind their kids, force their way into the childless couple's home and insist that the couple treat them to a sake party.

20 / *"Sister-Boys"*

ANOTHER area of Japan's *mizu shobai* which is peculiar if not unique is the role played by the country's ample collection of "gay" boys who in Japan are known as "sister-boys."* Here, where there are no legal or social sanctions to inhibit them, the "gay" ones really let their hair down, many of them dressing and acting like women in public as well as private.

* Like so many other words fashionable in Japan today, the term "sister-boy" was taken from an American movie (*Tea and Sympathy*).

Until recently, a large number used to appear nightly in an area next to Shimbashi Station in Tokyo, but most of them now congregate in some 41 "sister-boy" (S-B) bars—of which seventeen are located in Shinjuku Ward.

To the Japanese these bars are known as "Flowers of Evil," and because they are staffed by young men and boys, do not come under the anti-prostitution law. Most "gay" boys range in age from 18 to 25. Customers of such bars include middle-aged men (especially from the entertainment world), Geisha, cabaret hostesses (who are tired of men or are looking for men they can order around) and widows. Foreigners are regular customers at 30 percent of these bars.

A number of Japan's top entertainers are known sister-boys, and sister-boy roles are very common in popular entertainment. But some S-B's are so conspicuous in their dress and manner in public that even the tolerant Japanese are embarrassed.

For several Sunday mornings running, I had my weekly bowling session at the Tokyo Bowling Center pretty well snockered by the antics of one of Tokyo's better-known sister-boys who showed up with a famous male television star.

The S-B wore his hair fairly long and had it dyed a brilliant red. His usual costume consisted of skintight slacks and a completely transparent sport shirt worn outside his trousers. A frilly, black brassiere— fully visible—completed his ensemble.

It was not his attire, however that affected nearby bowlers. It was his manner of delivering the ball and returning to the bench. He didn't walk or strut. He minced. . .in a way that would make Marilyn Monroe blush.

Instances in which well-meaning visitors have been misled, you might say, by S-B's are fairly numerous. The S-B's who specialize in this are those who wear their hair shoulder length and to all outward appearances—if the light is a bit dim—are women.

Some look so attractive and so realistic that only a very close inspection will reveal the difference. Japanese girls (real ones) who compete with the S-B's in the same line of business, say that they scrutinize the suspect's throat, wrists, and feet. If there is an adam's apple and the wrists appear especially bony, they look at the feet. If the suspect's feet are noticeably big, they challenge said suspect to prove "her" sex or quit poaching.

An excellent illustration of how clever many S-B's are at impersonating women was reported in Nagoya just recently. A regular patron at a bar proposed marriage to one of the hostesses working there. The girl accepted, and later the happy man mentioned the good news to a friend who was also a regular patron of the same bar.

"That's not a she, it's a he," the friend exclaimed in amazement. The shocked lover immediately went to the bar and withdrew his proposal, but the disappointed "he" offered to become a "she" by getting an operation. The would-be groom blamed the whole thing on the fact that he is near-sighted but doesn't like to wear his glasses.

It is also rumored that some of the S-B's that still hang out in Tokyo's Shimbashi district are clever enough at acting like women that they are able to spend a night with a customer without him discovering their true sex.

One out of ten Japanese men is extremely effeminate in looks and manners when compared with the average male, but this is as much of a racial-social as a sexual characteristic, and newcomers should not to too hasty in hanging tags on milksop types.

21 / How To Be A Gigolo

WAGES in Japan are still based on age, longevity with a firm, and the number of dependents. This means that unmarried men in their twenties and early thirties are generally in the lowest income brackets regardless of their skill or ability, and they generally are not high enough to be authorized expense accounts. This means that their entertainment budgets are severely limited.

As a result of this economic situation, an exceptionally large percentage of young Japanese bachelors become *tsubame* or "swallows" (gigolos) when the opportunity arises. The opportunity arises fairly frequently for two reasons: There is a disproportionate number of widows and bachelor women in Japan because of the war, and because so many successful Japanese businessmen take young mistresses whenever they get about 40 years old, leaving their wives to wither or look for alliances elsewhere.

The majority of these wandering women, according to local newspapers and magazines (which carry extensive reports on the subject at regular intervals), confine their partners to high school and university students—who often appear ungrateful for this largess.

There are many, however, who have acquired a taste for foreign men, and restrict their depredations to susceptible and cooperative foreign bachelors on the town. One such lady, whose husband was at one time one of Japan's top financial leaders, was still very active the last time I heard, although she is approaching sixty.

Willing bachelors who attract this lady's attention are driven to and from their rendezvous in a large foreign car, treated to $50 dinners in exclusive Geisha restaurants and given expensive gifts.

Some of the women who fall into this category are found in social and cultural clubs with international memberships, where they are more likely to make the desired contacts. Most, however, are submerged in the life of the city, and it is necessary to move in strictly Japanese circles to meet them.

According to the testimony of several bachelors—

and acting bachelors—who have been on the economy in Tokyo for several years, the best way to promote this type of liaison is to set yourself up as an English teacher interested only in giving private lessons to well-to-do ladies. This is something like getting paid to eat your cake—if you don't mind your desserts well-done, that is.

One acquaintance who has had a very successful career as a *tsubame,* informed me that his most recent patroness owned a combination restaurant-bar and an apartment house, and for over a year provided him with all necessities, plus. It seems that he soured this set-up by inviting too many friends in too many times to share his paramour's bounty.

22 / Beware of Women Carrying "Hocho"

WOMEN everywhere have their favorite weapons for inflicting injury upon the stronger sex. In Japan, this weapon seems to be the *hocho,* a cross between a meat cleaver and a machete, found in most Japanese kitchens. This, of course, is not so different from the Western butcher knife, but here the similarity ends.

An American woman on the rampage with a butcher knife, will ordinarily be satisfied to stab her victim in the chest or stomach—or in the back if she's the shy type. The Japanese women, however, is prone to go after the offender's manhood and attempt to emasculate him, especially if she thinks he is interested in another woman. Since this requires more finesse than merely stabbing a body, the operation is usually performed when the patient is asleep or too drunk to defend himself.

The most sensational case of this type in recent years was actually not a premediated affair. A Tokyo businessman took his nymphomaniac mistress to Atami for what was intended to be a week-long holiday. Around the third night, the man was so tuckered out he couldn't function.

After several unsuccessful attempts to excite her partner, the woman hit upon the idea of pretending to emasculate him by making threatening motions with a *hocho*. She thought that psychological fear would act as a powerful sex stimulate. It did, and in her excitement she eunuched the man.

When found by the police a few days later, the woman had the results of her handy-work wrapped up in her furoshiki. Following a short period of incarceration, she was released and (fun-lovers take note) is now working in a *ryokan* in Tokyo's Asakusa district as a maid.

A case that made headlines a couple of years ago involved an American. One night the man confessed to his girl friend, with whom he had been living for two years, that he had a wife back in the U.S., and the wife was due to arrive in Japan shortly. After her lover went to sleep, the girl took a razor and cut off his *chimbo*. The man died, and the girl got off scott free, the judge trying the case ruling that she had given two years of her life to a man, who, all along, had been simply taking advantage of her.

Another example will crystalize this penchant for hitting a man below the bet. A short time ago, one of Hokkaido's largest coal mines was tied up in a strike. Union members formed a ring around the entrance of a mine facility by locking their arms together. So solid was this phalanx that repeated charges by opposition forces failed to crack it.

Finally, the wives of the men who wanted to get into the facility armed themselves with wirepliers, and on a given signal, rushed up and clamped down on the gonads of the strikers. You can imagine what happened to the invincible phalanx! The moral here: if any of your Japanese lady friends come at you with anything larger than a fingernail clipper, drop your guard.

23 / "Men With Brains Are No Good In Bed"

SHORTLY after arriving in Japan the first time, I noticed that the men who behaved in the roughest, most ungentlemanly way often made out the best with Japanese girls. As time passed, I found out why.

For centuries, Japanese women were conditioned to expect and accept the fact that their menfolk would be rough, vain, arrogant, and generally brutal, and any man who did not behave more or less in this manner was considered less than a man.

At the same time, the Japanese male was not all bore and brute. He also had an aesthetic side that complemented the poetic nature of Japanese girls, and saved him from being a complete savage.

This idea of expecting a man to be rough and demanding one moment and a poet the next is considerably weaker than what it was a few decades ago, but it is still very much in evidence among Japanese girls today—even though they feel compelled to deny it when it is mentioned.

The average foreigner in Japan would therefore appear to be doubly handicapped, since he has neither the aesthetic perception of the Japanese male, nor is he generally capable of the crude behavior still fairly typical of Japanese men.

But despite the fact that Japanese women were traditionally conditioned to accept this type of character and behavior, they were never so ignorant or naive to accept it as being preferred, and when the Westerner came along with his worship of the female, Japanese girls responded with a speed and alacrity little short of amazing.

Furthermore, one of the worst mistakes a foreigner in Japan can make is to attempt to behave toward Japanese women the same way Japanese men do. They will resist violently and if you persist, will treat you as if you just crawled out of some gutter.

It still remains, however, that the Japanese girl of today cannot deny a strong urge to be physically and mentally overwhelmed by her partner, and to the degree that if the man fails to overpower her, she will become spiteful and her feelings for the man concerned will be shallow and insincere.

This is especially noticeable among girls in the *mizu shobai* world who have experienced many men, and have gotten to the point where only an unusually masculine man means anything to them. The bookworm types usually get on their nerves and are not popular. I once heard a cabaret girl sum up the general feeling on the subject in one apt sentence. She said: "Men with brains are no good in bed!"

24 / The Girls Are Sentimental

BACK before Japan's legal redlight districts were closed down, two American bachelors of my acquaintance saved a lot of money and made a name for themselves in Yokohama by tricking girls in over a hundred of the city's houses. The two learned that Japanese girls, particularly redlight professionals, were intrigued by the idea of an adult male who looked and acted like a man but was still innocent. They also learned that by putting on an act of great shyness and reluctance to lose their pretended innocence, the girls would outdo each other to see who could "seduce" these unfortunate "male virgins" first.

The two were able to "operate" this way for nearly a year before their reputation caught up with them, and house madames started refusing them admittance.

Now that prostitution has lost its official sanction, and as a result has become a great deal more competitive, the girls in the business are not nearly so sentimental as they used to be. Some of the more money-minded, in fact, are apt to charge the novice more than the going rate. But, generally, the basic attitude still exists, and bachelors who put up an innocent front will find their reception more interesting if not improved in most circumstances.

25 / *Why Foreigners Like Japanese Women*

ONE OF the continuing marvels of every generation since West first began having intercourse with East is the attraction that Japanese girls exercise on Western men.

Many Western men, both the learned and the experienced, have attempted to explain this attraction, but none of the explanations that have come to my attention were complete. Everyone, it seems, is willing to grapple with the proposition, but none are willing to pin it down. The one common flaw in the judgments passed so far appears to be a conspiracy of reluctance to expose the weaknesses of women who, after all, do have many admirable traits.

My own image of the Japanese girl is that she is a sort of feminized "Picture of Dorian Gray;" a creature who has traditionally been shaped to serve both as a fragile decoration and a sturdy receptacle for man's ego. The fact that she actually succeeds to a considerable degree in fulfilling both these uses is a remarkable accomplishment.

When in her natural state—that is, un-Westernized and in a Japanese setting—the Japanese girl is about the closest nature has come to producing the type of imaginary women the average American male has on a pedestal. She has an innocent-appearing, baby-faced cuteness that is particularly appealing to Western men (because the average Western woman is far from cute in this way and it suggests youth, innocence, etc.). She is also small-bodied and delicate-appearing, like a young Caucasian girl of fourteen or fifteen years of age...and therefore has the appearance of "forbidden fruit" that is, however, accessible!

Most Japanese girls are also more graceful, petite, refined, patient, sensitive, and poetic-minded than their Western counterparts.*

* Japanese girls have traditionally been famous for their shy and gentle ways, and most of them deserve this reputation still today. But democracy is having its effect. Most of the country's hundreds of juvenile gangs include a sprinkling of girls, and occasions in which young girls engage in such activities as pick-pocketing, shop-lifting and extortion through threats of bodily harm, are becoming more frequent. The most interesting manifestation of changing

All of which combine to make Japanese girls, at first glance, appear the epitome of femininity and charm to Western males, And, so long as they are not removed from a Japanese setting, this description is valid enough. Trouble arises when any permanent foreign element is introduced into this idyllic scene. Since we are not interested in permanent relationships, that is another story.

The *piece de resistance*, however, is the factor that the average Japanese girl, along with her other feminine attributes, is more willing to prove her ultimate femininity than most of her Western sisters. No matter how pleasing the physical appearance or how intriguing the manners, the popularity Japanese girls enjoy with foreign men is primarily founded on the ease with which they can be had. All else is extra, like cake under icing.

Another reason why foreign men are often attracted to Japanese girls is that they pity them... with a pity that, when viewed from a certain angle, may feel like love. But much of this pity is selfish egotism built up by the individual foreigner who comes to believe that the girl is naive, soft, sensitive, and helpless, and wouldn't be able to live without him!

Japanese womanhood—and American manhood——to come to my attention in the last few months, occurred in Gotemba, a good-sized city about three hours southwest of Tokyo. According to police reports, several girl gangs in this city have recently been arrested for severely beating American marines from a nearby camp who refused to give them money or buy them drinks.

A further reason involves both a superiority and an inferiority complex on the part of the foreigner. Many Western men, particularly Americans, are never sure of their prowess with women (because of less opportunity to develop it, no doubt), and there is always the very great fear that they will fail and be shamed.

These people find, however, that where Japanese girls are concerned, they lose this sense of fear because *they feel inherently superior to them* and thereby need feel no shame. Where young men who had their first and only sexual experience in Japan are concerned, they are apt to become hypercritical of American women and irrational in their sentiments about Japanese girls.

The fact that a good ninety per cent of the foreign men and their Japanese girl friends cannot communicate with each other except on the most basic level also contributes to this mutual attraction in the early stages. Not being able to share an intellectual or cultural companionship, their relationship is primarily physical; a situation which would seemingly be made to order for modern man with all his neuroses.

Newly arrived bachelors who feel that kind fortune has brought them into an unspoiled paradise will generally not be disappointed so long as they are content with the icing.

While this is not intended to be a psychological treatise, there is one key psychological factor which has much to do with the popularity of Japanese women. In fact it is primarily responsible for one of the main characteristics of the Japanese, both men and women. This is the tremendously strong desire of most of the men to be mothered, and the need of most of the women to provide this mothering.

The tiny, flower-like wife treats her big, strong, drunken husband as a little baby. *Mizu shobai* girls treat their customers like they are little boys, allowing them to revert to such childhood freedoms as lewd, vulgar talk and taking liberties with the girls' physical charms.

As Japanese psychologists say, "Japanese men like to be cuddled, and this is the oil of love-life in Japan." The psychologists further explain that this inbred desire of Japanese men to be cuddled and treated like children by women is because they are lonely and embarrassed by being free and having no one to lean on. They are therefore particularly susceptible to being ordered around. Failing to find someone to order them around, the pendulum swings the other way and they became excessively dictatorial.

Complementing these strong desires in Japanese men, Japanese girls like to sacrifice themselves for men...in such a way that they have complete power over them. Japanese women need to have one or more men dependent upon them, otherwise they become frustrated and suffer a great deal. If a man is willing to give up all prerogatives to a Japanese woman, she will care for him like he was a child.

Foreign men find this mothering just as attractive as Japanese men—for short periods.

The foreign bachelor who has visions of latching onto a cute doll-like Japanese girl who will be shy, retiring, and submit to his every whim had better brush up on his female psychology. University of Hawaii psychologist Abe Arkoff recently made a study which showed beyond a reasonable doubt that American girls of Caucasian ancestry are more submissive to their husbands than Japanese girls are to theirs—particularly Japanese girls who are university educated. The most submissive of all the girls studied turned out to be Hawaiian girls of Japanese ancestry —who reflect the attitudes of a Japan that no longer exists.

26 / How Japanese Feel About Foreigners

BEING an isolated, ethnically homogenous country, the Japanese very naturally developed some rather startling national ideas about Westerners. Records say that the first Western Caucasians to set foot on Japan were three shipwrecked Portuguese cast upon Tanega Island in 1542, a little over 400 years ago.

The Japanese called these first foreigners, *gaijin* or "outside people." In the next few decades, other foreigners, including a number of Jesuit priests, made their way to Japan or were cast upon its shores by storms. Most of these earliest visitors were seamen who undoubtedly were not the most genteel type of ambassadors. It is said that a number of such arrivals were put in wooden cages and displayed in various parts of the country as examples of the savages that lived outside of the land of a million gods.

Several of these unintentional visitors must have been red-headed, immensely hairy—the sailors were no doubt bearded—and had long noses, that appeared more like beaks to the Japanese. The result of this was that foreigners came to be thought of and called *keto,* or hairy barbarian animals.

For in contrast, the Japanese were not hairy, they bathed regularly, dressed in refined, graceful costumes and conducted themselves according to strict formalized rules of etiquette that still today make them world famous. It was also said that the only things *gaijin* cared about were ravishing women and eating babies.

These attitudes, as stated above, are said to date from around the middle of the 16th Century when history records the appearance of the first Caucasian Westerners in Japan. It is my theory, however, that Westerners first appeared in Japan many hundreds of years before this. I believe the legendary stories of the *Tengu* have their origin in the presence of Westerners in Japan long before the beginning of the middle ages.

Tengu, known to every Japanese from childhood,

are "mythical" creatures who live in the mountains. They are classified into two types. One is man-shaped, with a long nose and lots of hair, and is generally pictured as having wings. The other appears in the shape of a crow-like bird. Their man-shaped leader has long mustaches and a long gray beard.

The *Tengu* are always evil, coming down out of the mountains to pillage and kill. They are said to have great strength, to be incredibly skilled swordsmen, and to be inordinately fond of strong drinks. In addition to their robbing, killing, and drinking, the *Tengu* are pictured as women ravishers and baby eaters.

A single band of Westerners, brought to Japan from whatever direction by plan or adverse winds and driven into the mountains by hostile inhabitants, could be the origin of this enduring story. At any rate, this is the general background from which the Japanese have traditionally looked at foreigners—and it suggests that foreign bachelors in Japan would have always been faced by a tremendous handicap whenever they attempted to approach a Japanese girl.

But, paradox that it appears to be, Japanese girls are drawn to foreign men and are so susceptible to them that Japanese social commentators have made this a popular subject. The reason for this is not at all hard to understand.

For centuries, Japanese women were oppressed by

their menfolk. Men were little gods and women their servants, with very few rights. Like it or not, women had to put up with vulgar, callous manners that were considered proper behavior for most men. When Westerners arrived with their ideas of chivalry toward women, Japanese girls very quickly learned that instead of being monsters, foreign men treated them like fairy princesses on little thrones; and they liked it.

A general analysis of what the Japanese think of Westerners today is interesting and enlightning. From personal experience gained in more than ten years of living with and among Japanese families, working with Japanese, plus making a number of studies of their likes and dislikes, I find the following to be generally true:

In Tokyo and other large cities, Japanese girls and women up to forty-five or so generally like foreign men and are spontaneously friendly. Women above this age are often surreptitiously hostile, particularly if they have pretensions of blue-blood. Women of all ages in the countryside are on the average exceedingly friendly.

With men it is a different story. By the time little boys are three years old they are well-indoctrinated with the idea that foreign men are natural enemies, and they tend to be suspicious and wary of foreigners they see in the streets.

By the time they reach school age, boys seem to overcome a certain amount of this early conditioning, which now is primarily through television and comic books, and often display characteristics of being frank and friendly. Somewhere around their twelfth year, however, they regain their animosity and hostility toward foreigners.

A favorite pastime of boys of this age, when they are in school yards or riding in buses, etc., is to yell obscenities and curse words, in Japanese, of course, at foreigners passing by. During one three-year period when I lived near an American military housing area, I used to stop on occasion and listen to young Japanese boys who would gather regularly at the same place and yell curses at foreign kids playing in an open field, for no other reason than to express a natural animosity toward them. At other times, Japanese students of both sexes are so friendly and outgoing that it can actually be bothersome.

Taken as a group, Japanese men are prone to dislike foreign men for half a dozen reasons mostly stemming from ignorance and a colossal inferiority complex. This dislike is usually well-controlled by all classes except young laborers, gangster elements, and Japanese "teddy boys," who make a practice of sneering or making belittling remarks at passing foreigners. If approached directly and mannerly on an individual basis, most of these people will immediately drop into the pose of extreme politeness characteristic of traditional Japanese behavior.

Naturally there are a great many exceptions to the above generalizations, and in almost every case where there is ill-feeling, it disappears or diminishes as soon as the individuals concerned have an opportunity to meet foreigners and get acquainted with them. This also generally applies to foreigners in their feelings toward Japanese men.

I remember very clearly my own experiences along this line. During my first few years in Tokyo, I rode the very crowded trains, subways, and streetcars on an average of five times a day. While jammed up sardine-tight with the other passengers, I used to catch myself looking at certain faces around me and hating them—for no other reason than the fact that they appeared hateful to me. Dozens of times, I had to drag my mind away from such thoughts and remind myself that if someone should happen to introduce me to the object of my "hatred" we would be laughing and joking within seconds.

The feeling Japanese men have for foreigners, although often complicated by more subtle, emotional considerations, is very much the same. Much of it is based on imaginary factors that disappear when exposed to friendly overtures.

On the day of this writing, however, an incident occurred in Tokyo which starkly illustrates the intense feeling many Japanese men have about things foreign.

A young bookstore clerk began conversing in school-English with a Japanese student friend he met on the street near his place of work. This so infuriated a 24-year old man standing within hearing distance that he picked up an axe that happened to be laying nearby and struck the bookstore clerk in the head with it.

This is reminiscent of pre-war Japan when anyone daring to show any sign of Western influence was liable to be attacked and in some cases killed on the spot by "patriotic" Japanese. This violent reaction is a reflection of the tremendous frustrations, some of which are brought on by their inferiority complex, under which most Japanese men live.

27 / "Foreigners Are Sex Happy"

IF THE foreign bachelor in Japan lives up to his local reputation, he will lead a very active life. The Japanese, particularly the men, believe that foreigners are as promiscuous as monkeys and as regular as rabbits. At the same time, they consider themselves paragons of virtue. Both men and women tend to be very modest when it comes to their own interest in sex.

I have had many Japanese women attempt to convince me that the hundreds of redlight districts that used to flourish openly throughout the country were patronized primarily by foreigners, and that the only Japanese who visited them were hoodlums and other degenerate elements.

The average Japanese male seems to have what

amounts to a neurotic interest in the foreigner's opinions of Japanese girls, along with his relations with them. The second question that Japanese men ask visiting foreign men is "How do you like Japanese girls?" (The first question is "How do you like Japan?"—which is generally asked before you have been in the country for thirty minutes.) Both questions are the result of their inferiority complex and an uncontrollable desire to hear something about Japan extolled.

Although Japanese men, particularly those in their late teens and early twenties, are prone to resent the idea of foreigners making time with Japanese girls— and often demonstrate this resentment in their behavior toward the girls concerned—they nevertheless appear to derive masochistic pleasure from seeing it and talking about it to foreigners.

Many have told me, however, that they couldn't understand why foreigners were so crazy about Japanese girls. They parrot the popular story that Japanese girls are the kindest women and make the best wives in the world, but they don't really believe this, and one of the great desires of most Japanese men is to try out a foreign girl (which explains the very great success of a number of foreign girls operating in Tokyo's Ginza entertainment district).

Their opinion of the licentious behavior of foreigners is, of course, based on fact. Finding themselves in a society where the pursuit of casual erotic experience is accepted, most foreigners lose no time in availing themselves. One reason why the Japanese are able to criticize foreigners for taking advantage of ample opportunity is simply because the Caucasion Westerner is so conspicuous in Japan, no matter how he conducts himself; and, of course, they do not measure themselves by the same standards.

28 / How To Approach Japanese Girls!

ONE OF the most common questions asked by bachelors newly arrived in Japan is: "What is the best approach to use with Japanese girls?" This is a loaded question but it can be answered in fairly specific terms.

First, however, let us divide the girls into seven general classifications. These are: (1) girls still in school; (2) the daughters of well-to-do families who do not work; (3) girls who work in ordinary offices or shops as clerks, etc.; (4) girls who work in coffee shops*; (5) girls who work in bars and cabarets; (6) girls who are members of the hot-rod set or Thunder Clan (Kaminari-zoku, as they are called in Japanese); and (7) girls who stand in doorways and shadows along the streets at night.

Not very many bachelors will be interested in girls

* There are some 8,000 coffee shops in Tokyo; 16,000 throughout Japan.

still in school, but for those who have a delayed penchant for liberal arts, a few comments are appropriate. First, most Japanese school girls are romantic to a degree that has to be experienced to be fully appreciated. They are extremely susceptible to intense infatuations which they take seriously...and wherein lies the danger. The best approach for the bachelor interested in school girls is, therefore, one that will take him in the opposite direction.

Next is category two, or girls from well-to-do families who do not work. Girls in this class are generally hardest to approach unless you can manage to get an introduction into their exclusive circle. Arranging this is no different than what it would be anywhere else. From then on, it's up to your personality and pocketbook.

If you are reasonably pleasant to both the girls and their male friends, and can pay your own way, you'll find the pace fast and friendly. Unless you want to limit your range, however, don't play any special favorites in public or you'll find yourself paired off for the duration. Romantically panned, secret rendezvous in some out-of-the-way resort are the thing here.

With a little practice, it is possible to tell whether or not a girl is from a wealthy family just by looking at her. If she is very well-to-do, she will most likely be tall and slender, and have attractive if not beautiful features. If she is from a family that has been wealthy and titled for several generations, she will very often look somewhat foreign.

Her dress will be stylish and obviously expensive, and her manners will be that of someone who is poised, confident, and knowledgeable. She very seldom behaves in the childishly coquetish manner so common among middle-class girls. If she also happens to be a graduate of one of the so-called Christian women's schools, she will speak fluent English and will be foreign oriented to the extent that she prefers Western style living *and* Western men.

Third are girls working in typical offices and stores, whose numbers seem limitless but who generally are the most uninteresting group of girls in the country. They are easy enough to approach—even with the language barrier—but they are almost always exceedingly sensitive to being approached openly in their place of work.

Best technique here is to find another girl somewhere in the same office or shop, tell her that you can't live unless you can meet Miss so-and-so (whom you point out or describe), and invariably the second girl, intrigued with the fascination of romance, will become your cohort and go-between and chances are, end up getting you a date fixed up for some nearby coffee shop. Again, generally speaking, this group offers the professional bachelor the least opportunity, and considering the amount of groundwork involved in establishing a relationship with them, is hardly worth it.

Next are the girls who work in the country's several thousand coffee shops, which are actually more like cocktail lounges that also serve coffee. This group deserves special mention because most coffee shops hire their waitresses (one for nearly every table in the place) on the basis of looks, with some shops going all out to hire the best-looking girls possible.

As a result of this practice, some of the most beautiful girls in Japan work in coffee shops, and many shops are nationally famous for the beauty of their girls. Such places pay what amounts to very high salaries to these girls, in some cases up to four times what they would be getting in an ordinary office job.

This combination of high salaries and the prestige of working in a shop noted for its beautiful girls tends to attract not only girls who are pretty but many who are very well educated and come from middle and upper class families.

Such coffee shops are naturally favorite hunting grounds for many playboys, both Japanese and foreign, and generally deserve their popularity. A special technique is also usually necessary to get acquainted with these girls, as they do not sit with customers and there is less opportunity to make the initial contact.

Here again, it is hardly ever advisable to approach a coffee shop girl directly while she is on duty. There are exceptional cases, but any attempt to date one of these girls within sight and sound of her co-workers and the other customers is almost certainly doomed to failure.

There are three simple approaches that are used regularly with respectable success. First is to have a diplomatic friend or go-between sound out the girl for you, or get you an introduction to her in a way that won't embarrass her, and follow this up with an invitation to go to another coffee shop or restaurant. To be the most successful, all this should be accomplished without anyone else in the coffee shop where she works knowing about it.

Next is slipping the girl a note directly or through a third person. This has limitations because many of the girls don't know enough English to understand more than a few words or sentences, like "I love you." Learning a few key Japanese phrases is the best solution; copying them out of a phrase book works.

The third system is to again enlist the aid of one of the girls in the shop. If you can get across, in English, sign language or Japanese, the idea that you want to meet one of the other girls, there is a very good chance that who ever you approach will help you. In a few of the more self-conscious coffee shops in Tokyo, the girls are under orders not to engage in conversation with customers. In shops like this, notes are necessary.

Category four, or girls who work in cabarets, bars, and clubs, provide no problem. They are hired to entertain customers, which they do by sitting with them, dancing with them and performing other types of "service" designed to get the customer to stay longer and spend more. Just about anything goes in cabarets, bars, and most clubs except the few name places that cater primarily to foreigners.

Meeting girls in the "Thunder Clan" is fairly simple—just do what they do and you'll fit in. Get yourself a motorcycle, a leather jacket, and tight blue jeans, and join the pack in their races up and down the better stretches of highway in and around the major cities.

The last category, girls who stand in doorways and shadows at night, can be approached by anybody who has the price—but many refuse foreigners for various reasons. Chances of being burned by a girl in this group are more than sporting, and it is best to steer clear.

In actual practice, it isn't always necessary for the foreign bachelor to make the first move. Many Japanese girls, particularly those working in the "floating world," are anxious to snare foreign husbands. But they are a lot more particular than what girls in similar circumstances used to be. Nowadays they prefer successful businessmen with large incomes and impressive living allowances.

There is also a growing group of girls who refuse to have anything to do with any except foreign men. There are others, from all classes, who are compelled by a strong urge to try a foreigner just once. Some of these women frequently accost foreign men in public places. One bachelor-friend in his late twenties, who Japanese women find unusually attractive, is approached so often by girls in their teens and twenties as well as matrons in their late thirties and forties, that he is something of a celebrity in Tokyo.

The most popular meeting place in Japan, for whatever purpose, are the ubiquitous *kissa ten* (coffee shops), which range in size from tiny, cave-like basement spots seating six to ten, to giant multi-storied affairs that can accommodate hundreds.

Businessmen, students, shoppers, and a large group of people who seem to have nothing to do, use the shops daily as an extension of their home or office. Some of the types of shops that have developed to cater to special segments of the population include the *midnight kissa*, which stays open most of the night; the *denwa* (telephone) *kissa*, which features a large number of phones for use by patrons; the *koshitsu kissa*, which has private booths for its customers and is therefore popular with couples; the *bijin kissa*, or "beautiful girl" shops, which are popular bachelor hangouts; the *nude kissa*, featuring waitresses in skimpy costumes; and the *jazz kissa*, which specialize in jazz music.

29 / Call Girls And "Date Clubs"

IN ADDITION to the pick-up bars, cabarets, and night clubs, there are several call-girl rings operating in Tokyo and other large cities. The system now in effect is practically law-proof and becoming more popular.

A madame or master establishes a club with two or more female members. The "club" then solicits male "members" through word-of-mouth, printed cards, and hand-bills passed out in entertainment districts or stuck under automobile windshield wipers.

Any man wanting to become a "member" and thereby earn the right to be introduced to a female member calls a listed telephone number. In most cases, someone at the other end of the line gives him another number to call, and the second number may give him a third before he is allowed to make contact.

Then, if he is not suspected of being a policeman, a club member makes arrangements to meet him at some coffee shop, collects an initiation fee of one to three thousand yen, gives him a membership card and then introduces him to a date. He usually has to pay the date from one to several thousand yen, depending upon her class (A, B, C, D, E), plus room and incidental expenses at a ryokan.

Female members of these clubs are made up of housewives, students, models, office girls, and coffee shop girls.

In Tokyo a number of the more active of these clubs are operated by girls who used to work at one or other of the city's top clubs as hostesses. Hundreds of girls working at less well-known bars and cabarets in Tokyo are part-time members of such clubs.

Date clubs that came to my attention as the result of a single inquiry included the "Chiyoda," the "Heiwa Kanko," and the "BG," all of which catered to men, plus two catering to women "who want to make friends with handsome boys": the Bar Sankaku and Club Yuki.

For current telephone numbers, all you have to do is inquire at most any bar or cabaret for the nearest date club, or look under the windshield wipers of cars parked in any of the entertainment districts.

Japan naturally affords the resident bachelor opportunities that the short-time visitor cannot possibly take advantage of. This does not mean that Japan has to be a dry run for the traveler just passing through. The girls of the "floating world" have traditionally paid special interest to men on the road because they are both more receptive and more generous.

Places and areas catering to clientele who are in this category—and therefore don't have time for elaborate campaigns—have changed, however. In cities like Tokyo and Osaka, these include a number of relatively small, intimate, and sometimes exclusive cabarets that are more like bars in appearance.

An example of this type in Tokyo that is anything but exclusive is the Bohemian in Shibuya Ward's Maruyama-cho, at one time a famous Geisha and redlight district. The Bohemian is narrow and dark and usually filled with smoke and loud, popular music. Its girls, who run to the fleshy, voluptuous type, are hustlers first and last. From the moment a customer enters, they are constantly after him to buy drinks.

A customer who doesn't want to wait until such bars close before getting together with the girl of his choice can bail her out by paying off the management. The rate varies but is generally around $6, which is over and above what the girl gets.

Once an agreement is reached, before the bar closes or after, the girls take their friends to an inn or some third grade hotel in one of the popular assignation areas.

The Lady Fair near Tokyo's Dai Ichi Hotel in Uchisaiwaicho, is similar to the Bohemian in operation, but is on a considerably higher level. The Lady Fair girls are carefully selected and managed by the bar madame, no arrangements are allowed unless the madame approves of the customer's character, and generally in order to be accepted by the madame, a customer has to have been introduced and vouched for by a steady client.

Known customers who prove reliable are allowed to charge their expenses at the Lady Fair, which makes this one of the few bars in Tokyo offering this service to foreigners.

Despite the popularity and abundance of erotic pleasure in Japan, however, it is not all that easy for the visitor passing through for the first time to make out on his own, simply because he doesn't know the ropes and doesn't have time to learn them.

As a result, many foreigners who live and work in Tokyo in occupations which require them to meet incoming tourists and businessmen, are regularly called upon to act as "recreational directors." Some handle more "customers" than full-time professionals. For all practical purposes, this system is the most convenient for short-time visitors.

30 / Girls & Gifts

MANY foreign bachelors in Japan start off on the wrong foot by buying personal gifts for girls whom they are trying to make up to or impress. This is very embarrassing to the average Japanese girl, and may have the effect of causing her to avoid you, especially if you gave her or tried to give her an expensive gift.

Unlike Western girls, particularly the well-to-do, who very often feel no special obligation about accepting gifts from men, even casual acquaintances, the Japanese girl will very likely think you are trying to buy her and will resent it. If she should accept a gift from you, she will feel compelled to give you one in return—to stay even with you, not because she also has ulterior motives.

If you visit her at her home or apartment, a non-personal type of gift, like fruit or candy, is appropriate, however, and will be accepted with good grace.

Gift-giving in Japan, like so many other facets of Japanese life, is a complicated, sensitive business that must follow prescribed rules, any breach of which is a serious social transgression.

Where girls in the *mizu shobai* are concerned, these rules may or may not apply, depending on the individual. Generally, if a *mizu shobai* girl likes you and would be receptive to a proposition, she will accept a gift readily. If she refuses a gift, the message is very clear. She doesn't like you well enough to pay for it.

31 / The Bachelor's Wardrobe

NEWCOMERS to Japan are invariably amazed at how well the average Japanese dress, and it has now got to the point where it is necessary for foreign visitors to pay special attention to their appearance, least they find themselves in a disadvantageous position.

This is a recent phenomena. The idea a few years ago would have been greeted with condescending laughter.

By the summer of 1945, very few urban Japanese had any decent clothing left. Most of the expensive kimono making up the primary part of every girl's wardrobe had long since been traded to farmers for rice and vegetables, or sold on the black-market.

The textile industry was one of the first to recover, however, and by 1949 was turning out cheaply-made Western style clothing in volume. But the newly emancipated women were not content with the shapeless sacks produced by inexperienced manufacturers, and began making their own clothing by copying fashions from Sears Roebuck catalogs and similar sources, on a massive scale.

By 1953, women's apparel was beginning to blossom in both styling and color combinations—although a girl in a red sweater or skirt was still in danger of being automatically labeled a whore. Men's clothing on the other hand, continued to look like it had been designed to keep them from looking human.

It was not until around 1957 that men's wear in Japan began to look like it had been made by design, and from that time on progress has been rapid.

The overall look of modern Japanese men's wear is European; a mixture of English, Italian, and French, with a few original ideas of their own thrown in. Only young men, however, seem to be concerned with their appearance. The older men wear suits and ties, but most are unaware or unconcerned with whether or not they fit.

Being very fashion conscious and progressive, Japanese girls appreciate good grooming in their male friends, and this particularly applies to foreign male friends, since the girls are already flying in the face of society by associating with "outsiders."

To make the best impression, the bachelor in Japan should at all times be immaculate and wear clothing that in Japanese is called *oshare,* which means strikingly stylish in a distinctive, modern way. Shoes, a vest, or any accessory that is unusually attractive will gain you valuable points with the girls.

32 / What The Girls Look For

As THE most prestigious of Japan's entertainment districts, Tokyo's Ginza sets the fashions and standards for the "floating world," and the girls who "work" the Ginza area are the most particular in their choice of clients.

The routine is simple but clever. Girls on the lookout for a customer stroll around the area, usually in pairs. When they see a couple of men wearing expensive-watches, belts or socks, and themselves are on the prowl, they catch their eye and wink or smile in just the right way.

The reason why the girls look for men wearing expensive accessories is because they are a sure sign that the men have more money than the average person, since such items are usually sold only for cash, whereas apparel like a suit or coat can be bought on time payment by anybody.

Japanese bachelors in turn have developed special techniques to cope with this situation. Since the girls generally do not give a potential customer the high sign until he has passed up and down the Ginza three times, the man who wants to be picked up strolls casually and makes a point of giving serious attention to expensive merchandise in the windows of exclusive shops. If the man is wearing something expensive, he makes sure that it is as conspicuous as possible.

33 / Don't Be A "Practicing Husband!"

IN THE United States it is not so easy for a bachelor to set up temporary housekeeping with whatever girl strikes his fancy. In Japan, however, this is customary and might be called the traditional Japanese version of "going steady."

Along with the advantages that this situation affords, however, there are some disadvantages and dangers which every bachelor should keep in mind. First, the word has somehow gotten around among Japanese girls that American men are faithful to sweethearts (but never to wives—unless the wives are Japanese) and they become exceedingly jealous and possessive once you start paying the rent.

Second, if you play house for more than a few weeks and then unilaterally decide to dissolve the union, the young lady concerned, nine times out of ten, will do one of three things. She will try to kill herself. She will try to kill both herself and you, or she will embarrass hell out of you in front of your friends and associates every chance she gets.

The biggest danger, however, lies in the subtle way in which she binds you up in a web of ties and obligations that all too often lead to the marriage section of your embassy. Instead of making an effort to keep her intimate association with you a secret, she makes sure that the word gets around. Before long, the association is formally acknowledged as existing by her friends and her parents, and, like it or not, you are her official *naien-no-otto,* or "practicing husband."

By this time, a strong case of domesticity and a gigantic guilt complex have so weakened your resistance that you begin to rationalize, and before you realize it you have convinced yourself that you should marry the girl regardless of consequences. Advice to the contrary merely strengthens your resolve. After all, you rationalize, it's your life to do with as you wish.

Because it is so easy to fall into the cohabiting relationship, it happens to some eighty per cent of all single foreigners who spend more than six months in Japan. The wise bachelor will avoid this situation as if it were the plague, for a number of reasons. The most important of which, for our purposes, is it would mean the loss of his freedom.

Many American men who felt they were in control of the situation, have convinced themselves that they could get in and out without getting messed up, but they generally are not worldly enough. Continental Europeans express surprise at how often Americans let Japanese girls get them into untenable positions.

One of the reasons why this happens to American men is that they bring themselves down to, or assume, the level and outlook of the girl concerned. This may be commendable from the viewpoint of common humanity, but it is usually fatal for other purposes.

34 / Just Tell Them You're Married

ONE OF the biggest handicaps facing foreign bachelors in Japan for long periods is, therefore, the danger of becoming too involved or tied down with one girl. The best way to avoid this is to make up a wife for yourself and tell the girls you are married.

Generally, this will not cramp your style (many *mizu shobai* girls actually prefer married men) and it provides a perfect out whenever you need it. A friend who has since returned to browner pastures, used to use the fact that he was married but temporarily cut off as a regular line. He would tell the girls that his wife was either pregnant or not in Japan, and wouldn't they please help him relieve the pressure. It is surprising how many were sympathetic.

35 / On Choosing A Traveling Companion

SOME foreign businessmen visiting Japan combine business with pleasure by acquiring a girl companion to accompany them around the country. In many cases, these girls act as the man's interpreter and guide, and are sometimes accomplished enough to perform the functions of a secretary.

If the visitor is in Japan for pleasure, a female traveling companion is a big improvement over the usual travel bureau guide. The businessman, however, should keep in mind that as far as his Japanese associates are concerned he is committing a grave social error.

No matter who or what the girl is, they are prone to consider her a *joro* that caters to foreigners, which is pretty low even for a whore. They put up with the situation because they consider that the foreigner doesn't know any better and to bring the subject up would mean a loss of face on their part because the girl is Japanese.

Their objection does not, of course, stem from any moralistic feelings. They merely disapprove of the time and method.

A majority of the girls who become traveling companions for visiting foreigners are from the *mizu shobai* world, but a few, especially where businessmen are concerned, were originally introduced as part-time secretaries. Some who become acquainted with businessmen who visit Japan regularly get themselves on a monthly retainer fee basis all year around.

Few if any of the girls in this enviable position stay at home and knit while their patron is not in Japan— they are not the stay-at-home type—so it helps if he is broad-minded.

All traveling-with-companion is not confined to Japan. A considerable number of well-heeled businessmen take their Japanese girl friends abroad with them. Friends and acquaintances who travel a great deal say they regularly meet girls from the top three Tokyo night clubs in such places as New York, Cairo, Paris, and other world capitals, all traveling as somebody's personal secretary.

36 / Fun On The Trains

MANY Japanese men and not a few foreigners in Japan have long taken advantage of the crowded transportation system to fondle fellow female passengers who are jammed up against them and cannot move. The men know that the average girl or women will not make a scene because she is so reluctant to be embarrassed—or else—and this more often than might be suspected—she herself enjoys the experience. In fact, this once essentially male pastime is on the verge of being usurped by women. According to statistics released by the Tokyo National Railways, 53 per cent of those "committing indecent acts" on crowded trains are now *chijo* or female perverts.

Commenting on recent magazine stories about the growing number of *chijo* in Japan, columnist Kyoko Baba quoted a well-known Waseda University professor as saying the phenomena should not be surprising "since women are now equal with men in exercising their human rights". The professor goes on to say that regardless of whether it is intellectual" or not for so many women to gain sexual release in this way, they are driven to such measures because their desires are not fulfilled by their husbands or, if single, by socially-approved contact with young men.

Because of the prevalence of such conduct on trains by both men *chikan* and women *chijo*, railway companies now maintain staffs of security officers to "protect" other passengers. When a pervert is apprehended, his or her only punishment is to be taken to the station office and asked to write out an apology for such behavior. The concern demonstrated by the railway companies for the morals of their passengers is a relatively new thing, and is not exactly popular with male commuters whether they are *chikan* or not. The men, it seems, don't really object to being played with by *chijo* and would prefer that the railway companies keep their noses out of it.

Two examples quoted by Miss Baba reveal other interesting factors pertaining to erotica in Japan:

"One morning a 30-year old saleswoman was in the act of playing with a 27-year old man who was hanging onto an overhead strap in the crowded train coach. The man was obviously enjoying the experience. Then a 23-year old office girl sitting in front of the man noticed what the woman was doing. The office girl immediately screamed: 'Look everybody!

That woman is doing something funny!' Then the office girl jumped at the woman (nobody knows why). The woman promptly kicked the office girl hard with her high heels and tried to escape when the train pulled into the station. But she was caught by a railway security officer who had to turn her over to the police after he learned she had injured the office girl."

There is at least one foreign woman among the chijo operating in and around Tokyo. This one, a 38-year old American, is very popular among men who commute from Isogo to Tokyo every day. She has been taken into custody once ,at which time she promised to stop the practice. But she is still at it and the railway security officers have no authority to stop her.

"Said one of the officers: 'Because she does it in such a humorous way, which is characteristic of for-eigners, men cooperate with her to some extent, al-though with a sardonic smile. So we cannot do any-thing about her. Her victims are insensible to the fact that they are being victimized.'

"Testified one of her 'victims': "Her act isn't too vulgar or distasteful. When she is on the train our trip to Tokyo becomes rather enjoyable."

The woman herself was quoted as saying: "I mar-ried an Oklahoma farmer. Since he was killed in a traffic accident a year ago I have had neither hope nor dreams. I was still young and lonely. Yet I was too proud to become a plaything for men in my home country. While I was thus smouldering from discontent my friends who came back from Japan told me about their thrilling experiences on Japanese rush-hour trains. I now live in Yokohama, and my only enjoyment is to feel Japanese men while riding the Keihin Line every morning."

37 / Miscellaneous: The "Meibutsu" of Kumamoto

BACHELORS who find themselves in Kumamoto Prefecture in the center of Kyushu island may want to pick up a little of the area's *meibutsu*, or most famous product, as a souvenir. Herbally speaking, this most famous product, known as *zuiki* in Japanese, is a potato-like root which has the appearance and feel of soft hemp after it has been processed.

It is used as a sex implement by women and a sex accessory by men. A well-known Japanese expression, *zuiki-no namida* (tears of zuiki), infers that anyone who uses *zuiki* will cry with pleasure. A word of warning to bachelors who might contemplate the joys of *zuiki,* however. When dampened, the ring-shaped accessory swells quite a bit, and more than one hasty visitor has required the services of a surgeon to remove his accessory with a knife.

Because sex has always been such an important area of pleasure in Japan, it has long been considered a kind of universal art which deserved cultivating. This attitude remains in Japan today. A former musician turned doctor-professor has, in fact, recently succeeded in raising the act to the level of a concerto.

The professor's theory is that there is a certain rhythm necessary before love-making can be successful, and to make it easier for novices to develop this rhythm, he has set it to music.

Instead of the usual musical notes, our professor uses one type of sign to represent the male and another type for the female. All the "musicians" have to do is assume the positions illustrated by the symbols and move according to the beat arrangement. If this is done, the professor guarantees complete satisfaction.

39 / Miscellaneous: Wedding Charts

IN OLDEN Japan it was customary for newly wedded couples to be presented with a chart illustrating, in life-like full color, the forty-seven most popular love-making positions or techniques. This was done it is said, because the young couple were supposed to be innocent of all such knowledge, and the chart was an important factor in making their marriage a success.

This custom is no longer formally followed among urbanites in Japan but it has not disappeared from the scene. The only change in many areas is the manner in which the chart is presented, it now being the practice to more or less slip the chart to the couple in a surreptitious, humorous way.

Such erotic paintings and drawings are not considered pornographic or filthy by the Japanese. They appear regularly in magazines and books that are on public sale everywhere, and no effort is made to keep them hidden from children. In fact, the average Japanese child at the age of three knows more about the birds and bees than the average ten-year old American child.

One acquaintance, who left Japan several years ago, once told me an interesting story involving a forty-seven position chart. He was living with a nineteen-year old girl at the time in a spare bedroom on the second floor of the girl's home. One Sunday morning he and the girl were aroused from a late sleep by the girl's two younger sisters, aged eleven and thirteen.

The young girls had a forty-seven position chart that they had dug out of the family trunk, and wanted their big sister's boy friend to tell them which of the positions he liked best.

WOMEN in most countries equate hairiness—to a certain degree—with manliness, and Japanese women are not exceptions. In fact, the idea that hairy men are more virile is particularly strong among Japanese women...apparently because Japanese men are especially deficient in this category.

At any rate, Japanese girls invariably make a big fuss over any man who has hair on his chest, and they get a tremendous kick out of running their fingers through it. Foreign residents of Japan who are so endowed are not long in grasping the special advantage this gives them, and many of them play it for all it's worth.

Hirsute bachelors might keep this in mind, since it makes a sure-fire conversation piece, and often saves time as well. If you happen to be the type that has hair on his back, however, it is best to keep it to yourself. You'll get the same *sugoi ne!* (isn't that something!) reaction, but few of the girls will be as anxious to run their fingers through it.

41 / Don't Do As The Japanese Do!

THE FOREIGNER in Japan be he a bachelor in pursuit of pleasure or a businessman trying to earn a living, will get further if he does NOT do as the Japanese do. This may sound paradoxical, especially in the light of some of what has been said so far, but it is nevertheless true. Japan is one country in which the old adage "When in Rome..." runs counter to commonsense.

There are some areas and times when adhering to this rule is practical and pleasant, but these are primarily restricted to minor social amenities and personal habits, which do not involve matters of business or deeper social relationships.

The "Japanese Way" as such is opposed to abruptness, frankness, direct action, and most of the other manners characteristic of Western behavior. It is, instead, based on an extremely subtle etiquette which in so many cases is far removed from present-day reality, and requires an inbred knowledge to live within.

In the second place, few if any foreigners, no matter how versed they may be in the "Japanese Way," are capable of conducting themselves or their affairs according to Japanese concepts. Not being able to think and act like a Japanese, the foreigner cannot expect to do as well or compete with the Japanese when using their methods on their terms...and this is over and above the fact that most foreigners cannot communicate with the average Japanese except through a Japanese interpreter.

A third consideration is the interesting fact that the Japanese do not expect, and very often do not want, foreigners to behave in the Japanese way. This peculiar circumstance derives from the very strong Japanese belief that their "way," while beyond the understanding of outsiders, is also not good enough for foreigners.

There is also the feeling that any foreigner who makes an effort to behave strictly in the Japanese manner is both usurping a right that is exclusively Japanese, while condescendingly lowering himself at the same time.

As a result of these and other attitudes, the difference between the treatment given by one Japanese to another and that reserved for foreigners is remarkable, and is one of the most important reasons why foreigners, both visitors and residents, are so attracted to Japan.

In almost all circumstances, foreigners, no matter who they are, are treated like Very Important Persons by all Japanese, with a great deal of the extra service and servility that this can imply. In contrast, the Japanese are prone to treat each other with outward respect but little real consideration.

Therefore, when the foreigner attempts to behave in a strictly Japanese manner he generally mixes the Japanese up. They don't know whether to go ahead and treat him like an outsider regardless of his behavior, or pretend that he is Japanese. On the average, they treat him like a respected guest who is soft in the head.

My own personal experience, which has often been very painful, as well as the testimony of my foreign friends and business associates who are intimately familiar with life in Japan, indicates that the best approach is that of the "professional foreigner," or one who conducts himself in the best traditions of the foreign visitor (no matter how long he has been in Japan), abides by his own principles of good behavior, and respects but does not try to copy Japanese manners and ethics.

The foreign bachelor who attempts to be Japanese is depriving himself of many advantages, not all of which are unfair. The most important advantage gained by foregoing Japanese behavior is the tremendous amount of time and effort that is not wasted in ceremony and jockeying to maintain a false sense of harmony.

To complement the advice to "Put your best foot forward and be yourself," I would like to summarize by suggesting a number of "don'ts."

(1) Almost every Japanese girl has a sad story. And some are sadder than others. Unless you are the Feiffer-type that gets a kick out of being a crying post, don't give any girl a chance to tell you her troubles. If you do, she will immediately begin to treat you like big brother and father combined. Before long, she

is no longer an exotic, exciting, desirable woman. She is a poor girl who deserves something better than the life she lives, and you will be very tempted to help her get it.

(2)   Don't hide your intentions from a Japanese girl under any circumstances. They are exceedingly sensitive and tender in many ways but cruel and callous in others, and have a terrible tendency to put men in embarrassing positions when it is least expected. A favorite weapon is a suicide attempt.

(3)   Don't let a cabaret, bar, bathhouse, or date club, etc., stick you with a girl you don't want. If you get a hag and don't complain, you will be stuck with her for as long as you patronize the place.

(4)   While most men will automatically select the prettiest girl when there is a choice, there is a special consideration to keep in mind when girl-choosing in Japan, particularly if you plan more than a passing affair. When the time comes to end the affair, the attractive girl will be more apt to accept the separation and not go off the deep end. The plainer the girl, however, the stronger and more violently she will resist the break-up, even if the man is a dog and she, in fact, doesn't even like him. She knows that her chances of getting someone else are slim, and it is the nature of Japanese women that they need a man.

(5)   Don't forget to dress sharp and be neat. The Japanese are hypersensitive to clothes and cleanliness. One colleague who used to wear his old leather-elbowed school sweater to work was known (behind

his back) as "the foreign beggar" *(gaijin kojiki)*.

(6) Don't ever raise your voice if you have a difference of opinion with a Japanese. If you do, it indicates that you are angry, and the Japanese concerned is therefore honor-bound to stand up to you so as not to lose face. If you remain calm, he will be more apt to apologize if he is wrong; and sometimes if he is right.

(7) Don't discuss personal or private affairs in Japan's cabarets, clubs, and bars. The girls have keen ears and are great gossipers. It is also wise to keep your voice down while in hotels. The rooms, even in name hotels, are not soundproof.

(8) Be careful about demonstrating your affection or friendliness to girls in public (by patting them or putting your hands on them). This is enough to convince any Japanese who sees the action that the girl concerned is a *joro*. She may not be, and you may not care what people think; but she does.

(9) Don't expect every girl you meet to be accessible. There are two kinds that are not. Those who really mean it when they say no, and those to whom your money and foreign face mean nothing.

(10) Don't talk loud, don't brag, don't swagger when you walk, don't display large sums of cash, don't be crude when offering a tip or present, don't stare hard-eyed at young punks (they consider it insulting and an invitation to fight), don't get mad at taxi drivers who won't stop to pick you up or bars that won't let you in (there isn't a thing you can do

about either one, and you may as well save your
stomach for a vice that satisfies), don't forget that
Japanese men are responsible for making Japanese
women what they are.

GLOSSARY

CONTRARY to popular opinion (entertained by all Japanese and most "outsiders") colloquial Japanese is not difficult for foreigners to learn. No ordinary person is goink to become fluent in the language in three weeks, or three months for that matter, but it takes only a few minutes to pick up a vocabulary of key words, the use of which will make your stay in Japan considerably more interesting.

For just that purpose, I have included here a list of terms that are especially meaningful in the world of the *mizu shobai,* along with a phonetic pronunciation guide. All you have to do to pronounce the Japanese correctly is read the phonetic version as if it were everyday English.

Chonga (chown-gah) —A bachelor who has had no sexual experience.

Ni-go san (knee-go sahn)—A second wife, literally, "Mrs. Number Two."

Danna (dawn-nah)—In traditional usage, husband or master. As used by *mizu shobai* girls and house madames, it refers, rather obsequiously, to any man who is out on the town. "Waka," meaning "young" is ofen prefixed to *danna* when the reference is to a very young man.

Suke (sue-kay)—Vulgar slang for girl friend.

Shike komu (she-kay coe-moo)—To go to a hotel or ryokan with a girl friend.

Zagin-no chan-ne (zah-geen-no chahn-nay)—Ginza-no ne-chan said backwards and meaning a mizu sho-bai girl who works on the Ginza.

Ueteru (way-tay-rue)—sex hungry.

Iichatsuku (Ee-chah-t'sue-coo)—Literally, to come together and bother or rub against. In colloquial usage: a "love hotel" where you can take your girl friend.

Furu (Foo-rue)—To fall out of love with a girl and cast her aside.

Kechinbo (kay-cheen-bow)—Someone who is stingy, a tightwad.

Aokan (ah-oh-kahn)—To engage in sex under the open sky, from "ao" for blue and "kan" for sleep.

Aibore (aye-bow-ray)—An unlucky word in the "floating world," aibore means a kiss between real lovers. It also means sashimi, or raw fish.

Akashisenko (Ah-cah-she-sane-coe)—A word meaning to pay an all-night fee (called "hanadai") at a Geisha house, from "akashi" for the breaking of morning, and "senko" for the incense which used to be lit to keep track of the time at an entertainment house.

Agari (ah-gah-ree)—Literally to rise or go up, this

word is used to mean tea to avoid saying *cha* (tea) which is bad luck in the "floating world."

Asagomi (ah-sah-go-me)—To drop in for just a few minutes to see your favorite prostitute early in the morning. Also used to refer to the practice of young toughs employed by houses of ill-repute to sneak in for a quick visit after the all-night customer leaves in the morning. The word literally means "morning-bother."

Aburamushi (ah-boo-rah-moo-she)—In the mizu shobai world, the boy friend of a Geisha or prostitute. Actually a cockroach.

Zakone (zah-coe-nay)—A gang-bang between several men and women, from "zatsu" for many, "uo" for fish, and "ne" for sleep.

Tsu or *Tsukyaku* (t'sue or t'sue-k'yah-coo)—A word used to describe anyone who knows a lot about the mizu shobai, from the Japanese word meaning to commute regularly.

Naki o ireru (nah-key-oh ee-ray-rue)—To make crying noises during the sex act in order to cause the customer to finish more quickly and get the process over with.

Himo (he-moe)—A tough who hangs around a prostitute to get part of her earnings. They sometimes rob customers; protect the girl from drunks, etc. Himo are common in Tokyo's Asakusa area and growing more so in Shibuya and Shinjuku. There are few if any on the Ginza.

Oshibori (oh-she-bow-ree)—Generally a dampened hand-towel given to newly arrived guests at inns and restaurants to wipe their hands and face, but also used in the mizu shobai to mean taking a customer for everything he has, from the word to milk or squeeze.

Ochazuke (oh-chah-zoo-kay)—A girl who sleeps with a friend of her best customer, from "tea" and "to soak." Also a popular food.

Ochabintsuki (oh-cha-bean-t'sue-key)—A man who takes his wife along and walks through a redlight district making fun of the prostitutes, literally someone who takes his own teapot along.

Hashigonomi (hah-she-go-no-me)—An expression which means to visit several drinking places consecutively on one drinking spree. Literally "ladder drinking," or getting higher and higher by going from one place to another.

Donchansawagi (doan-chaan-sah-wah-gee)—"Don" and "chan" are onomatopoeic for "bang" and "crash." Sawagi means to make a loud noise with the mouth, by talking or singing. Altogether, the three words mean a good time at a bar or cabaret.

Ikasu (ee-cah-sue)—Appealing, fascinating, romantic, lovely, handsome, etc., to the Nth degree. Used as an adjective by both sexes to describe people or things that really impress them.

Guttokichatta (goo-toe-key-cha-tah)—To be struck dumb by the beauty or looks, etc., of someone.

Kamatoto (Cah-mah-toe-toe)—A person, usually a girl, who pretends to know nothing about sex. Girls working in bars and cabarets will often do this because it makes them appear far more attractive to men.

Patoron (pah-toe-roan)—The Japanese pronunciation of "patron," which, when used in Japan, means a man who keeps a girl or woman, usually financing her in some business venture like a bar, beauty parlor, or restaurant.

BG—The letters "BG" are short for business girl. In Japan this means a girl who works in an office or factory, not a B-girl.

Himo-tsuki (he-moe-t'sue-key)—A girl who claims that she is single but has a husband or lover with whom she lives, the connotation being that this type of girl is dangerous to play around with. Literally, someone who has strings attached to them.

Muzu muzu suru (moo-zoo moo-zoo sue-rue)—To become sexually excited; used in the same way as the English word "hot."

Doan Fuan (Don Juan)—A lady-killer.

Gochisosama (go-chee-sow-sah-mah)—The standard

Japanese term used to express appreciation after eating, or being dined. Also used to express envy, jealousy, etc., when someone tells you about their love adventures.

"H" (pronounced "aa-chee")—Short for "hentai" or abnormal, this expression is used by girls to describe or admonish a man when he gets fresh by pinching, fonding, or making an unusual suggestion.

Aibiki (aye-bee-key)—A date with a sweetheart or lover.

Borareru (bow-rah-ray-rue)—To be over-charged at a drinking place.

Kawaigaru (cah-wah-ee-gah-rue)—Originally used in reference to taking loving care of children, now also used by men when they want to offer complete physical satisfaction to a woman.

Wetto (wayt-toe)—The Japanese pronounciation of "wet," which is used to describe someone who is sentimental, kind, warm-hearted, and unselfish, in some cases to a slightly excessive degree.

Dorai (doe-rye)—Someone who is "dorai" (dry) is not sentimental, is very business-like and tends to be hard-boiled, but is not necessarily a bad character.

Yokkyufuman (yoe-que-foo-mahn)—The state of being frustrated, usually sexually, and most often said of women.

Iyarashii (eeyah-rah-she)—Used constantly by girls

to express annoyance or disgust, sometimes strongly but more often in a teasing, joking manner when resisting (half-heartedly) the advances of men or reacting to suggestive remarks.

Joji (joe-jee)—A genuine love affair.

Shokku (show'coo)—Used primarily by young girls to express their feelings when they meet or see an especially attractive man, from the English word "shock."

Junjo (june-joe)—Unspoiled; usually used in reference to a man who has had no experience with women and is girl-shy.

Onna doraku (own-nah doe-rah-coo)—A playboy whose only object in life is to have as many women as possible.

Uwaki (ou-wah-key)—To be fickle, to go from one girl to another, to cheat on your wife or sweetheart. A very common word in the mizu shobai.

Cho-cho (choe-choe)—To flit from one girl to another like a butterfly, from the Japanese word meaning butterfly. Now common usage because it was easy for Occupation GI's to pronounce and understand.

Katai (cah-tie)—Often used to describe a person who is the serious, stay-at-home type.

Katagi (cah-tah-gee)—Someone who is not "mizu shobai." This word is interesting because the mere fact that it exists indicates just how important the mizu shobai was (and is) in Japan.

Tai atari de (tie-ah-tah-ree-day)—To use your physical assets aggressively to accomplish an end or make one's self popular; often said of hostesses and bar girls who habitually use their body to get ahead.

Sabisu ga ii (sah-be-sue-gah-ee)—This literally means that "the service is good" but as used in the mizu shobai it means that the girls in a bar, cabaret, Turkish bath, etc., are especially skilled at pleasing customers.

Dotei (doe-tay)—A male virgin. Mizu shobai girls often tease men who are shy or have an innocent look by calling them dotei.

Shojo (show-joe)—A female virgin. Mizu shobai girls will often claim to be shojo just to heighten their customer's interest. An increasing percentage of girls who are "katagi" (not mizu shobai) resent being referred to as shojo, and are apt to describe experiences that they actually have never had.

Onna-girai (own-nah-gee-rye)—Someone who hates or pretends to hate women. Sometimes used to infer that a certain person is "gay."

Koibito (coy-be-toe)—A very good Japanese word meaning "love person" or sweetheart.

Renai kekkon (rain-aye-keck-cone)—A love marriage, now becoming fairly common in Japan, particularly among couples in their very early twenties.

Miai kekkon (me-aye keck-cone)—An arranged marriage, still the most common type in rural Japan, and among couples who are in their late twenties and older in all parts of Japan.

Yoromeki (yoe-roe-may-key)—Literally to lean toward something, in this case a love affair, usually illicit. Also used in the past tense—yorometa. This word was first used to describe older women who stepped out, but it is now used without special reference to sex or age.

Kisu (key-suc)—The Japanese pronounciation of "kiss," which is now more commonly used than the Japanese word for the same idea (seppun—"sayppoon).

Hana-no shita ga nagai (hah-nah-no shitah-gah nah-guy)—Literally, "beneath the nose is long," or "the lip beneath the nose is long." A common saying used to described a man who is girl-crazy, or a man who will do anything a girl asks because he loves her blindly.

Futsuka yoi (futes-cah yoy, as in "boy")—Something that is good for two days, i.e., a hangover.

Bakajanakaroka! (bah-cah-jah-nah-cah-row-cah!) A rather weak version of "crazy S.O.B."

Suezen kuwanu wa otoko no haji (sue-eh-zane coo-wah-new wah oh-toe-coe no hah-jee)—A popular Japanese proverb which translates loosely as: "If a girl offers herself to you it is a slap in the face if you don't oblige her."

Omekake (oh-may-cah-key)—The colloquial Japanese term for "mistress."

Otoko date (oh-toe-coe dot-tay)—A good-looking man who dresses stylishly.

Jodan (joe-don)—Japanese for "joke."

Mara-kyodai (mar-rah k'yoe-dye)—A common term used to describe two or more men who have been intimate with the same girl. "Mara" means the male organ and "kyodai" means "brothers."

Obenjo (oh-bane-joe)—Literally, "honorable convenient place." Figuratively, a toilet.

Soha (sow-hah)—Abortion. Abortion is legal in Japan, and *soha byoin* (abortion hospitals) abound all over the country. Cost per operation is from $6 to $20.

Yoru-baito (Yoe-rue by-toe)—A new word meaning to work part-time at night, or, in the noun form, a person who works part-time at night. As used it refers to girls who hold down regular office or store jobs during the day, and then join the *mizu shobai* at night, generally on the sly.

Danmo (don-moe)—Modern jazz.

Naon (nah-own)—*Onna* (woman) said backwards in Japanese.

Saten (sah-tane)—slang for coffee shop.

"S" (pronounced "Esu")—The new "in" term for "sex."

Tsurekomi-yado (t'sue-ray-coe-me-yah-doe)—Love-making hotel or inn.